D0340323

Playing for Paterno

One Coach, Two Eras

A Father's and Son's Personal
Recollections of Playing for JoePa

Charlie Pittman and Tony Pittman

as told to Jae Bryson

TRIUMPH
BOOKS

Copyright © 2007 by Charlie Pittman, Tony Pittman, and Jae Bryson

No part of this publication may be reproduced, stored in a retrieval system, or transmitted in any form by any means, electronic, mechanical, photocopying, or otherwise, without the prior written permission of the publisher, Triumph Books, 542 South Dearborn Street, Suite 750, Chicago, Illinois 60605.

Triumph Books and colophon are registered trademarks of Random House, Inc.

Library of Congress Cataloging-in-Publication Data

Pittman, Charles Vernon, 1948–
Playing for Paterno / Charlie Pittman and Tony Pittman ; with Jae Bryson.
    p. cm.
ISBN-13: 978-1-60078-000-4 (alk. paper)
ISBN-10: 1-60078-000-8 (alk. paper)
  1. Paterno, Joe, 1926– 2. Football coaches—United States. 3. Penn State Nittany Lions (Football team) 4. Pennsylvania State University—Football. I. Pittman, Charles Anthony, 1971– II. Bryson, Jae, 1962– III. Title.

GV958.P46P58 2007
796.332092—dc22
[B]
                                                                  2007008355

This book is available in quantity at special discounts for your group or organization. For further information, contact:

Triumph Books
542 South Dearborn Street
Suite 750
Chicago, Illinois 60605
(312) 939-3330
Fax (312) 663-3557

Printed in U.S.A.
ISBN-13: 978-1-60078-000-4
Design by Chris Mulligan
Photos courtesy of the Pittman family unless otherwise indicated.

This book is dedicated to the memory of our family dogs, Nittany and Spike. Loyal and caring, their love never faltered.

To Lenny Moore, who impacted my life in a positive way—more than he would ever know.

To every defensive lineman who ever blocked for me. I could not have made it in football without you.

To the late Bill Reese of Centre Hall, Pennsylvania, who was my biggest fan.

Contents

Foreword

It has been 37 years since Charlie Pittman played for me, and I remember his career as if it were yesterday. When I recruited Charlie, I recall being impressed by his father, an honest, earnest man whose heartfelt desire was a good education for his eldest son. Since that time, I have had the pleasure of meeting most of the family: Charles's wife Mauresé, his daughters, and, of course, Tony and his wife, Tega. It is a special family, and I think Charlie and Tony's time at Penn State helped forge something special— not just for their family, but for the university as well. Charlie and Tony were my first players who were father and son, and we are forever bonded by that fact. Charlie became one of the strongest team leaders I ever coached, and Tony exhibited a determination and intelligence that I knew would one day push him to the heights of the business or political world.

I often quote the poet Robert Browning, particularly his work "Andrea del Sarto" and the line, "A man's reach should exceed his grasp, or what's a heaven for?" Both Charles and Tony do something wonderful—they strive. They learn from their failures and their successes. They epitomize Browning's line. Both are great examples of what I expect from student-athletes in my program. As players, they understood that crossing the Blue Line meant they had to be prepared for whatever my staff and I had in store for them. Not once did they ever back away from that challenge. They were fearless competitors during their playing days, and they are fearless in the business world. The fact that they were both undefeated as starters doesn't surprise me. They were excellent players on teams full of excellent young men. I am pleased that they want to share their memories of the Nittany Lions program, and I am just as pleased that they want to sprinkle some of their business acumen amidst those memories. I think any careful reader will find inspiration in the words of this book.

—*Joe Paterno*

Foreword

I often speak to students, mostly on college campuses. Many of them want the road map to becoming what I have been, the general manager of a National Football League club. I tell them there is no road map. Like me, they must figure it out on their own, find their own way.

What I say to all of them is that there was one indispensable stop on my career path, and that stop was the Pennsylvania State University. I probably could have grown up in another town, received my undergraduate degree from a different university, worked for different newspapers, and still might have made it to the top positions in the National Football League. I am convinced that without Penn State, without spending a little more than a year working for the athletics department of that university, I would not have made it.

Why? Yes, it is a wonderful university with a great setting, a great ambience, a terrific student body, and prestige. But the simple reason for my success is the people I was with. At the top of that list is Charlie Pittman.

Charlie was a star halfback on the 1968 and 1969 teams when I was the assistant sports information director. We connected during those years. In the time since, we have stayed in contact as our positions have changed and as we grew in our respective industries. Two years ago, at a reception at Penn State celebrating Lydell Mitchell's induction into the College Football Hall of Fame, Charlie and I commemorated a friendship that I have cherished for close to 40 years. Charlie told me how appreciative he was that, despite the number of athletes I have been around in the NFL, he and I have always been able to stay in communication with each other. I told him, "Charlie, I've been in football for 35 years (at that time). No experience meant more to me than my years at Penn State. And no bond of friendship meant more to me than yours."

If I had to choose one word to describe Charlie Pittman it would be *elegant*. He has an elegance of character. Elegance of style. Elegance of intellect. Elegance of morality. I feel privileged to have him as a friend, and it has been a joy for me to watch what he has done with his life. Yes, he was a football star, and I often say he made the greatest five-yard run I have ever seen to score against Syracuse in 1969, when it seemed our undefeated streak was going to end. But more important than that, I am so proud of him as a man, a husband, a father, and a successful businessman. And how wonderful it is that he and his son, Tony, can tell their stories together.

Collectively, they played in 45 games at Penn State during their respective college football careers. Both played on teams that had perfect seasons (Charlie in 1969 and Tony in 1994). Unfortunately, although both teams were the best in the country in those years, neither team was voted the national champion. That 1969 Penn State team featured two National Football Hall of Famers, Franco Harris and Jack Ham. It featured four first-team All-Americans in 1969, including Charlie Pittman. And it included a host of College Football Hall of Famers.

I truly believe that had it not been for an unfortunate injury on the opening kickoff of the second game of Charlie's senior season, against Colorado, Pittman would have won the Heisman Trophy. It is apparent on film that a Colorado player grabbed Charlie's ankle and twisted it. Afterward, calcium deposits set in at the injury site, and the ankle was never quite the same. However, this gave Charlie a chance to display even more of his greatness because, despite the injury, he still led Penn State to a perfect season and a second-straight Orange Bowl victory. He was still selected first-team Kodak All-American.

The injury, however, dropped Charlie's NFL draft selection to the third round. He played for St. Louis for a few years. Then in 1972, when I was the public relations director of the Baltimore Colts, with virtually no influence on player personnel, I nagged our head coach, Don McCafferty, into claiming Charlie when the Cardinals placed him on waivers.

The Colts were training in Tampa, Florida, that summer and were not covered by all of the Baltimore-area media. Consequently, I was the media stringer. Every afternoon I would call every Baltimore media outlet that wasn't represented in Tampa to report how impressive Charlie Pittman was. What great runs he was making. How he was playing his way onto our team. I wasn't being dishonest, but I will admit (35 years later) to a slight bit of exaggeration.

McCafferty began hearing about my reports and angrily approached me. He said, "What are you doing to me? The way you're publicizing Pittman, how can I cut him?"

I said, "Mac, don't cut him. He should make the team."

Which he did. I believed in Charlie as a player, and he deserved to make that team.

I loved Charlie Pittman as a friend, and I have for all these years. It is a friendship that I have cherished for 38 years. How appropriate that he and Tony can tell their stories together.

—*Ernie Accorsi*

Acknowledgments

Charles and Tony: The love of a father and son who shared the common love and respect for the same college coach—a father figure for one and a grandfather figure for another—from whom they both learned the value of being a team player and having a thirst for success, and life lessons on how to win with others.

Thank you to our wives, Mauresé and Tega, for sharing memories and enduring those countless hours when our thoughts were on the book and not on what was being said in our "wives' idle chatter."

Charles: Pam Abdo, for urging me to write the book, and the patience of Jae Bryson.

Tony: We've all heard the saying, "There is no *I* in team." Those who have played for Coach Paterno know how true that is for all who have worn the Blue and White. When I visited a Penn State practice during the 2005 season, I happened to get a chance to speak with Joe between drills. I mentioned that together my father and I had gone 45–0–1 as starters on his teams. At first he said that he didn't believe it. Then, after a few seconds of thought, he said, "Well, there were a lot of pretty good players on those teams, you know." Agreed. Not only were there many great players on those teams, there were many great young men whom we watched and emulated as we learned how to win. Without them, our teammates, this story would not be possible. For it is through them that we learn the many valuable life lessons of football—the ultimate team sport. Therefore, it's my teammates I would like to thank for making this book possible.

Introduction

"People always come up to me and ask me which one of my football teams was the greatest. I tell them to ask me 20 years after my last one plays so I can see how many CEOs, teachers, doctors, or lawyers they go on to be."

—PENN STATE COACH JOE PATERNO

Joe Paterno's football field is significantly larger, in his mind, than it is for most. Rabid fans, painted in the colors of their favorite teams, see 100 yards of green mayhem. Paterno has always seen something more: a runway to a better life for 100 Penn State football players each year.

And there have been a lot of years. Paterno became the Nittany Lions' head coach in 1966. Put into perspective, less than half of the world's population even existed when he first put that whistle around his neck.

And there have been a lot of players. If you subscribe to the *It's a Wonderful Life* theory of cause and effect, Paterno's players have treated football fans to some of the most magnificent moments in sports history. Using the George Bailey equation, without Paterno, there is no Franco Harris to catch the "Immaculate Reception"; without Paterno, there is no Lydell Mitchell to turn the Baltimore Colts around; without Paterno, eastern football remains an intramural sport; and the phrase "Grand Experiment" becomes a marketing campaign for New Coke.

Paterno is larger than football because he has always measured his success by something larger—the contributions of his players to society *after* their football-playing days.

The roughly 4,000 former Nittany Lions collectively are doing well. Certainly, there are NFL players—more than 200 of them over the years, including Lydell Mitchell, Franco Harris, Andre Collins, Kerry Collins, John Cappelletti, Larry Johnson, and more. Just as importantly, there are CEOs (Bob Holuba, Franco Harris), doctors (Carl Gray, Dave Joyner), dentists (Bill Lenkaitis, Bob Capretto), real estate developers (Don Abbey), NFL honchos (Matt Millen), corporate executives (Charles Pittman), and corporate up-and-comers (Tony Pittman).

Any book about Joe Paterno is beggared by the depth of a man in his eighties who successfully coaches a young man's sport and requires—no, demands—that his charges do something more in their lives than make a tackle or run a ball.

"You have to believe, down in your heart, that you are destined to do great things," Paterno often says.

Thus, a book about "Paterno's boys" by definition has to be about more than football. It has to be about life. Charles Pittman, Paterno's first All-American running back and his first African American recruit, understands that.

"For years, people have asked Tony and me the same question," Pittman says. "What's it like to play for Joe Paterno?"

Tony is Pittman's son, and both men have a singular perspective on that question.

"Sportswriters, reporters, authors, sports information directors, radio announcers, all have written books about Joe Paterno and Penn State football," says Charles. "Never has a former player written a Penn State football book. We think former players can best answer the question of what it is like to play for Joe Paterno. Tony and I started on three out of five of his undefeated teams; we were the first father and son to play for him— I was in Paterno's first class and Tony was in his [27th] class; we both were Academic All-Americans. It has been almost 40 years since I last scored a touchdown, and Joe's coaching is as relevant to me now as it is to Tony. We both epitomize the essence of what it is to be a part of the Penn State program and the Grand Experiment."

Through the prism of the Pittmans' experiences, the lessons of Paterno color both their football and business worlds. That, then, is the starting point.

Like a good football coach, this book will bolster your courage by explaining football and business, winning and losing, in a way that will help you understand all four things better than you do now. In the process, you might just change your life—because that's what these entwined concepts and entities can do, they can change your life for better or worse. In Paterno's world, understanding football is no more or less of an accomplishment than understanding chess or balance sheets.

Most important, your guides for understanding football and business success are men who know the paths well. There are three men at the heart of this book. Paterno is one; the other two are football greats Charles Vernon "Charlie" Pittman and Charles Anthony "Tony" Pittman.

Charles Pittman is an executive with Schurz Communications, Inc.; Charlie Pittman is his younger self (Pittman made a conscious effort to be called Charles after his playing days ended).

Tony is a supply chain executive with EDS in Plano, Texas.

Both Charles and Tony were elite football players who played at Penn State during two critical eras of that program—its ascension into a major program in the mid-1960s and its mid-1990s glory years after winning two national championships. It is their hope that after reading this book you will possess the power to craft winning marketing strategies, winning sales strategies, winning...well, you get the picture.

It is unique that neither Charles nor Tony ever lost a game as starters at Penn State. Just as Paterno did for the Pittmans, this book will point you in the right direction so that you may achieve your own undefeated seasons in your chosen profession.

There won't be much rah-rah in the instructions to come; if you're not already excited by what you do, perhaps you should rethink your career choice. There will be lots of Penn State football stories, business suggestions, and inside looks at elite businesspeople and athletes. Great coaches and great players lead by example—everyone knows that. The question is: are you prepared to learn from these football-flavored examples?

Being undefeated is an end result by definition, but you should be aware that the process varies wildly. Whether victories are achieved in a series of squeakers or blowouts, wins are wins. You will come to appreciate that the balancing act of winning and losing is a thing of beauty. It is a bouquet of *W*s sprinkled with illness, comebacks, infirmities, and bad officiating.

It is something you have within your power to achieve.

Time is not an obstacle, just in case you've already begun doubting your ability to change. Athletics in general, not just football, are full of miraculous achievements. For instance, in track and field, Roger Bannister was a man of singular purpose. He was the first man to run a mile in less than four minutes. In a testament to the power of planning, he trained for that iconic mark with daily workouts that fit into his university class schedule.

Bannister cracked a barrier no one else in the world had surpassed by jogging 10 minutes to his local track and running 10 400-meter sprints at a 60-second pace, with two minutes of rest between sprints.

Counting the 10-minute jog back, Bannister established what was then considered an unbreakable world record simply by instituting a regularly scheduled 48 minutes of work. That's slightly more than a coffee break for most people.

Such breakthroughs are possible in athletics because elite athletes continually strive to break barriers. Sports editor Ron Bracken agrees that Bannister's single-minded, well-planned drive for success is reflected in the attitudes of prized football recruits, another type of athlete who does amazing physical things in between classes.

Bracken is a legendary sportswriter for the *Centre Daily Times* newspaper in State College, Pennsylvania. He has been a journalist for nearly four decades, and it's safe to say that he's probably met as many football recruits as most college coaches while covering the Penn State program. He sees a common thread in those who succeed.

"They have amazing self-confidence," Bracken observes. "They believe in themselves. They say, 'Go ahead, put me in the toughest situation you can and watch me succeed.' They feel they are good enough to do whatever it takes to meet a challenge. They can handle it."

Charles starred as a crafty, outsized running back on a defensive-minded team, while Tony shone as an undersized defensive back on a high-powered offensive team. They were both starters for powerhouse programs. They were the best at what they did on the best teams in the nation. Neither ever walked away from a challenge; each always wanted to play against world-class talent.

Charlie Pittman never lost a game he started in high school, and neither man ever lost a game they started at Penn State.

Their combined college records are 45-0-1. In the sports world, that is a miraculous number. In football, there is no father-son tandem better at their game, recordwise, than the Pittmans.

In football and in business, these men know what it takes to be undefeated.

Former New York Giants general manager Ernie Accorsi has spent decades guiding NFL teams—the Baltimore Colts and Cleveland Browns, in addition to the Giants. He guided the Giants to Super Bowl XXXV, orchestrated two NFC East Division championships, and made the deal that brought talented young quarterback Eli Manning to New York. Accorsi knows football, and the Pittmans' record surprises even him.

"It's unprecedented; it's hard to believe," Accorsi said. "Sure, [Penn State] got some raps on [its] schedule. But that record for a father and son at the same university—and the son played in the Big Ten—that is something mind-boggling."

Besides football prowess, the business lives of Charles and Tony offer lessons for everyone. Charles is a self-made man who came from humble beginnings, and he is closer to the end of his career than to the beginning. "Self-made" is a term Charles is not very comfortable with; he feels his success bears the handprints of dozens of men and women. But the fact is that he came from a home in which money was scarce. There were times when the electricity was cut off and the family endured cold nights. It wasn't a world that proffered high-level business connections. He came to the business world later than many men his age because of his NFL career with Baltimore and St. Louis. With a young family to support in the early 1970s, Pittman spotted most of his peers from the class of 1970 a two-year head start before he entered the business world.

Tony is a 34-year-old who was born into privilege—the child of an executive. He went to a prestigious prep school and turned down opportunities at Harvard, Princeton, and Yale to attend Penn State. Physically, most people notice Tony's smile and ramrod-straight posture when first meeting him. Tony possesses the baritone voice of a radio announcer and a stunt pilot's confidence. Like his old college coach, he hates being underdressed. Tony is as comfortable in a suit and tie as he is in jeans. When it came time to consider the NFL, he chose instead to work at Fortune 500 companies and never looked back.

The choices they make and the challenges they face in business run the gamut. In many ways they are polar opposites in their sports and business careers, with one notable exception—both are considered winners by any reasoned estimation.

They are family-centered men who carve out time for their wives and children, they are well-compensated, they are in positions to make decisions important to their companies, and they are well-respected by both peers and subordinates and their former coach.

And, of course, there's JoePa.

Paterno is one of those amazing human beings who make normal people shake their clocks in frustration, wondering if he gets the benefit of a 25-hour day. Besides winning national championships in football, Ivy League–educated Paterno has one of the highest graduation rates of any Division 1A program and has donated millions of dollars of his own money to Penn State University.

Either Pittman could have been anything he wanted to be—world-class tennis player, high-tech entrepreneur—but the intricacies of football, with its 35-mile-per-hour ballet of impacts, called to both men. It was Joe Paterno, one of the game's most astute judges of talent, who showed them the way. Between the three, you have the gold standard in planning, success, and winning.

The strategies offered in this book are an amalgam of the Pittman, Paterno, and Penn State systems. Their methods comprise a playbook of information that resonates with anyone who wants success in any field. There are suggestions to sharpen surveys of your competition, methods to improve your own discipline, rules for creating your "team" of champions, and, most important, tried and true strategies to set goals so you don't have to ever second-guess how well you're doing.

This is your chance to see the inner workings of success; a chance to become a virtual 12th teammate on some of the best football teams in history. This is an opportunity to access the combined wisdom of Charles and Tony Pittman—and Joe Paterno.

Call it the Tao of the Three Ps.

If football's not your game, but you're looking for help in your day-to-day business dealings, don't put this book down.

As the Pittmans and Paterno know, if you understand the principles of business, football, winning, and losing—and how they relate to one another—you will be able to manipulate them to your advantage. And soon your corner of the business world will be the champagne-drenched locker room of your imagining.

If you want to be the undisputed champion of your industry, read on. The great thing is that the concepts you need are hiding in plain sight, a road map to success that needs only your "aha!" to commence the journey. Are you in sales? Perfect! Manufacturing? Wonderful! Consulting? Great! Are you a manager? A CEO? A new employee? Good, good, and good!

We are going to talk, like friends, about football. But you should translate every football lesson into a business lesson. Every down should speak of ROI; every yard should speak of career advancement. The goal line is your personal business success—the collective touchdowns of your own undefeated season.

Success. That is what this book aims to describe for you in action-oriented detail. Everything is included, except the smell of the locker room.

Your winning season will start as all winning seasons do—on the recruiting trail. So before you read a word about Penn State football, your assignment is to understand the recruiting process.

The recruiting process forces one to objectively evaluate the skills of another—just as Paterno once evaluated the Pittmans' skills. It's not an overstatement to say Penn State's success hung in the balance with those long-ago choices.

Had Paterno attempted to turn Charlie into a defensive back by misreading his skill set and his psychological makeup, he would have lost him to a more astute recruiter. Charlie Pittman was a crucial cog in the Penn State pantheon. He was the first running back recruited by Paterno, the first All-American back of Paterno's head coaching career, and if he hadn't gotten Charlie's commitment, there is a strong possibility that future Penn State star running backs Franco Harris and Lydell Mitchell might have gone elsewhere. That would have created an entirely different history for Penn State, all because of a slip in the recruitment process.

If you're not knowledgeable about high-stakes recruiting, at least know this: the formalized courtship of the recruitment process is often viewed by outsiders—those who have never been recruited for a college team—as a one-way process. The gifted young player is wooed and dined (if not wined) by college coaches. If the wooing works, then the player is won over.

But that is an oversimplification.

In addition to the hundreds, sometimes thousands, of hours spent by college recruiters in researching each candidate, there is research done by the young recruits themselves. *What conference do I want to play in? What does the television contract look like? Will I start right away? Who plays my position, and what year is he? What was the team's record last year? How many players have been sent to the pros?*

These are just the preliminary questions a player might ask. After all, both parties stand to lose much if the fit is wrong: a poor choice would cost the university in the pricey neighborhood of $100,000 for a full-ride scholarship. The young man could lose an opportunity to play professionally if his physical skills and emotional needs aren't adequately developed in a college setting.

Why is it important to understand the recruiting process? It's crucial to know that the stakes are high early in any process. By selecting a fast team rather than a big team—as Paterno did for his 1966 defensive recruits—strengths and weaknesses are set. That is a lesson for football and life.

Another thing to know about Joe Paterno and the Pittmans is that they are fiercely punctual. The first thing any of them say to anyone who walks up to them and asks how he can perform better in his field is, "Have you made a commitment to always being on time?"

It is a cornerstone of their success—showing up at the right time.

At the website www.communicaid.com, foreign business executives are given crash courses on how to assimilate into American business culture. At the top of that list of suggestions and observations is this sage counsel: "In the U.S., punctuality is an essential part of business etiquette and, as such, scheduled appointments or meetings must be attended on time. Americans perceive lateness as a sign of disrespect."

The Pittmans and Paterno couldn't agree more. Height, weight, bench press, or foot speed may make a player—but it's all for naught if that player's not ready to consistently show up for the game.

Be early for appointments, recommends Penn State class of 1993 free safety Lee Rubin. Rubin knows a thing or two about success and preparation. As a sophomore in 1991, he led Penn State in tackles with 60; 45 of those were solo tackles. Rubin is now an entrepreneur and a Sunday school teacher.

"Being on time is about discipline, structure—toughness. It's all business," says Rubin. "I really believe that Joe—consciously—wasn't just preparing us for Saturday's game, he was preparing us for life. That's not a football thing, that's a life thing, that's a family thing. I teach a Sunday school class at my church now. I tell the kids that being late is a big deal.

"Joe used to give us laps if we were late for meetings, one lap for each minute. He said if you were a minute late, you owed him 120 laps. The reason for that is the guy who's late owes a minute to each of the 120 people on the team—players and coaches."

If you are judicious in choosing how you spend your time and if you are consistently punctual for your appointments, you are what's known a "blue-chip recruit." If you're not, that is where you need to be—so fix it! Without the discipline of punctuality on your side, you are not a blue-chip prospect. At best, you're known as a "project," and that is not a desirable tag.

If punctuality is not your thing, you may be thinking the next paragraph will offer you suggestions on how to straighten that problem out for you.

You'd be wrong.

Football and business are for big people. If you can't find the will to be on time, this path is not your way to success. This book is a road map, not a crutch. Elite athletes don't operate from a "can't" mode. And there are minimum requirements before they can go further in their athletic career. Recruiters know that.

Like most major universities, Penn State has recruiting down to a science. Recruiters look at dozens of athletes each season and rate them on attitude, coachability, level of competition, commitment to the game, and, of course, physical talent. At the end of that exhaustive search for blue-chip recruits, Paterno himself will show up in their parents' living rooms and present his case.

By the way, if you haven't heard Paterno speak, it's an experience. He retains his Brooklyn accent after more than 50 years in Pennsylvania, and his voice is high and scratchy. Motivationally— going by his voice alone—Paterno ranks somewhere between your local deli proprietor and the dry cleaner down the block. But if you're on the receiving end of a recruiting pitch, he sounds like James Earl Jones.

Why? Because Paterno knows talent and has little time to waste, and his recruits know that. His presence in their living room validates their own high estimations of their abilities.

Above all, Paterno is an honest man who wants to do what's right by young people and by his program. That's Tony Pittman's take.

"I've got memories of Joe that go back as far as my father," Tony says. "As we went through the recruiting process, he told me, 'It really feels like I'm recruiting my son.' And he said it like he meant it. He told me he was good friends with [Yale's football coach] Carmen Cozza and said that going to Yale might be good for me. I've got to say that he really struggled. In my case, having known my father and me for so many years, he didn't just have the Penn State goggles on. He wanted to help define what was best for me beyond football."

Be like Joe. When analyzing yourself, think about where you want your talents to take you. More important, don't inflate your skills (or, in the language of football, don't lie about your speed in the 40).

For both Tony and Charles, even with athletic careers 25 years apart, simply getting into the game is not the full first step—and it shouldn't be yours. The objective is to think deeply about how you can achieve success. Charles often says that the most powerful tool a person has is the ability to say "no." Too many people allow that power to be usurped by their own kindness or by being unrealistic about the necessary level of involvement in a project.

Paterno has crafted a life out of sometimes saying "no." Most times, it has worked well. For example, he is virtually unreachable during the football season so his legendary attention to detail isn't sidetracked. Before you embark on a business goal, make sure it's the one you want. At the very least, ask these questions:

> Does it fit at this point in your life?
> Will you have the time to devote to it?
> What will it take to achieve it?
> When do you want to achieve it?
> What will it cost to achieve it?
> Is achieving it a worthwhile outcome?
> What are the positives that come with reaching your goal?

Let's now step into the shoes of Joe Paterno—because that's who you are in this phase of the process. You're the head coach sizing up your team, your competition, and your chances for success.

Recruiting Lesson One: Assess Your Skills in the Context of Your Team

Paterno is not alone in his ability to judge talent and use motivation. Even as a teen back in his hometown of Baltimore, Maryland, Charlie Pittman was an astute observer of team dynamics and situations. In fact, it was a survival skill. His parents taught him and his siblings that their name stood for something, and wasting God-given talent would never be accepted under their roof.

"There was no late-night carousing for the Pittman kids," he recalls. Their mother and father wouldn't have it. In order to avoid trouble on the streets of an inner city that was beginning to deal with an influx of drugs, increasing crime, and broken families, Charlie learned how to gauge not only situations, but himself and others as well.

Paterno recognized that talent, in addition to the young man's ability to break through a line of scrimmage.

Charlie Pittman hitting a hole in the offensive line was a thing of beauty, according to teammate Lydell Mitchell, who would go on to his own success as an All-American running back in the early 1970s. Tall and gangly, Charlie had a deceptive running style that evoked another tall and gangly superstar, Mel Farr, who attended UCLA from 1963 to 1967.

When Charlie hit a hole it seemed like he was able to do magic tricks with his 6'1", 180-pound frame. If an onrushing tackler expected him to follow gravity's rules and go down, he went up; left became right, and sure hits became definite misses. And then there were the afterburners. Charlie hitting a hole was a Miles Davis riff—creative, pulled from the moment—but Charlie getting past the line and into open field was a Dizzy Gillespie solo—fast, straight, and a joy to witness.

For Paterno, Charlie was a must-have blue-chipper. Paterno had inherited Coach Rip Engle's team in 1965, and in checking his cupboard noted that he had an iron-clad defense and a reasonably strong offensive line. What he needed from the class of '66 was speed—and leadership.

Having done as you've done—surveyed his team, his competition, and his chances for success—he must have salivated at the prospect of landing young Charlie Pittman. Charlie fit his needs like a key in a lock—a fast, talented, schoolboy All-American who had leadership capabilities. As a first-year coach, having a strong leader in the huddle, one who had bought into his philosophy, made Paterno's job easier.

Paterno was assessing not just what his team needed at the moment, but he was also looking to the future of his program. Because his defense was so strong, he knew he would be able to win games if he upgraded key offensive positions—and running back was a particularly crucial component. He had reviewed Charlie's skills and found them to be a match for what he felt his team needed.

You must do the same within the context of your career needs. If you feel like you are the right person in the right program, then the recruiting process is a success and the heavy lifting begins.

Here, a Penn State axiom will come in handy:

Recruiting Lesson Two: All Things Being Equal, Mental Toughness Is What Wins Games

When it comes to business success, the real lesson of sports is mental preparation. There is a Zen mystique surrounding gifted athletes that nonathletes often find hard to fathom. Paradoxes such as "The game slows down and comes to me when I'm in a zone," or "My game improved when I stopped thinking and started playing" are rampant in sports. Charles has another paradox that he applies to sports and business: "People think football is about knocking people down; it's really about helping people up."

That is the spirit of the winner. Your job—in addition to your listed job duties—is to help people up in a business world gone topsy-turvy.

The work begins now. You can be undefeated in life, but it means expending effort; it means teamwork, it means rules, it means planning. Just like spring football in Happy Valley (the bright, shiny nickname for State College, Pennsylvania), it means setting goals.

"In every sport, goals and standards are set. It's like a business operation," Charles says. "You need to know if you're doing well. If you don't know what to measure yourself against, you don't make progress. When you have goals and standards, you know who the better teams are, who leads the league in rushing. You're able to keep an eye on other competitors. You see how you measure and stack up against the standards and goals you set.

"If you can't measure it, you can't manage it. You have to measure and manage it. If you're a running team, for instance, you need to know how your running game is doing. Measurements help you understand how you're moving against the competition: am I better than I was last year? You have different metrics to help, benchmarks that tell stories about how well you're performing."

Recruiting Lesson Three: Know Who's Best in the Field

As you begin your planning, there are two things you must do first. One is to look around to see who is best in your chosen field.

Who was the "national champion" in your business last year? Define that however you want, but it's imperative that you do define it. In other words, which company was the best? What made it the best? Was it sales volume, sales growth, team development, or customer service?

Define it. Better still, define it by writing it down in super-specific terms that would make anyone say, "Oh, I see why XXY Company is considered the best." As you define the national champion of your field, you will also be defining the game you are playing.

Recruiting Lesson Four: Set the Season

Too often the average American will "set a goal" of losing weight. Or "set a goal" of quitting smoking. What they've actually done is make an open-ended promise to themselves that on some future date they will do those things. High performers are specific about their timeframes, their "seasons," so to speak. Set your season. Know with certainty what the first day and the last day is. You can be certain that the goals Tony and Charles Pittman set have "seasons." Both men speak precisely about what needs to happen by the end of the fiscal year—a precise date. Or what needs to happen by the end of the quarter—a precise date. Be it a calendar or fiscal year or six months or three months, human beings need seasons. Without seasons, there is no comparison, no champions, and no real competition. Seasons, artificial though they may be, delineate the moments of our lives and allow us to compete and compare.

A season may be defined as the time you've allotted yourself to attain your goals. If you are looking at career advancement, it is helpful to think in terms of years.

Or if your industry focuses on November and December sales, you might prefer to break the year into two six-month seasons. One season, in this example, might deal with completing all the preparations to place you and your business in the best position to take advantage of the end-of-the-year sales rush. That season might end in June. Its goal would be related to preparation, such as making 10,000 square feet of warehouse available for end-of-year inventory. The second season would then be the sales season. Winning that season might be about fattening the business accounts.

Okay, you've done four things: a) assessed your skills, b) committed to be mentally tough, c) defined the best team in your field, and d) set your season.

With those actions, you can almost smell fall in the air and hear the cheering crowds. Let's see where the football seasons take us.

PART I

Set Your Goals without
Second-Guessing

CHAPTER 1

Introducing the Pittmans

" I had no intention of going by the name Charlie after my playing days were over," says Charles Pittman, senior vice-president of Schurz Communications, Inc. "I didn't want to be known for scoring touchdowns."

If he did choose to use that as a calling card, his 33 touchdowns and career 4.9 yards average per rushing attempt would be among the top efforts at Penn State. Baltimore-born Charlie Pittman led the Nittany Lions in rushing for three straight years and was the top rusher (706 yards on 149 carries and 10 touchdowns) in a historic 1969 backfield that also included Hall of Famer Franco Harris and NFL Pro Bowl player Lydell Mitchell.

His son Tony proved just as dangerous on the other side of the ball. For those in the know, Penn State's 1994 football team was an offensive juggernaut that featured stars Ki-Jana Carter and Kerry Collins. Pittman's unit wasn't on the glamorous side of the ball in 1994, but his cerebral play at cornerback led to a respectable 39 tackles and an interception, following up a 1993 campaign in which he led the Nittany Lions with five interceptions. Like his father, he was undefeated in every game he started.

Their family legacy begins at 824 Appleton Street in west Baltimore, young Charlie Pittman's hometown.

Jean Pittman's husband, Charlie James Pittman, was always at work in the steel mills, so it was up to her to run herd on her children, especially her second born, Charles Vernon. The child was always fidgety; he seemed forever on the move. It was a lucky thing her oldest, Rosalind, just 10 months older than Charles Vernon—an Irish twin—was so precocious. It gave her another pair of eyes to keep watch over Junior and younger brother Jerome.

Charlie was a good student with very good grades, but most of all, he loved running. He ran to school. He ran to the library, the store, and everywhere he could.

He made a game of running as fast as he could on the edge of a curb to see how long he could go before losing his balance and falling off. While other 15-year-olds were outgrowing imaginary friends, he began inventing imaginary tacklers who would force him to swerve and spin as he ran. Or he would dodge cars or pick up cans as he ran. Baltimore police officers once ran after him because they thought he was doing something wrong. He wasn't. He was just running like he always did.

He was the running man of the family and the neighborhood. Rosalind was the smart one; she soaked up knowledge like a sponge and challenged Charlie to do better in school. Their brother Jerome was the quiet one; he studied voraciously. He would later earn valedictory honors at his high school.

The Pittmans were living through tough times. Around the close-knit family, the city of Baltimore had begun a precipitous decline that would make it one of the most dangerous cities in the United States by the end of the century.

Like many other west Baltimore families, there were times the few dollars they made were not enough to cover all their basic needs. There were a few winters when money was too tight to pay the heating bill, so the power company shut it off until it was paid. One of Rosalind's teachers chose that time to visit their cold, dark house to ask Mrs. Pittman to allow Rosalind to participate in a citywide spelling bee. Charlie knew it would be good for his big sister; he considered her the smartest person he knew. The teacher also thought highly of Rosalind and believed she could win the contest.

"No, Rosalind's not going to be in a spelling bee," Jean Pittman said. "She doesn't have nice clothes to wear for something like that."

Rosalind's disappointment welled up in her eyes and slid down her cheeks.

That's just not fair, Charlie thought. It seemed to him that Rosalind always had to sacrifice more than her younger brothers. He didn't care for spelling bees, but it was competition, and he wanted his sister to experience that joy.

He couldn't get enough competition. He lived for it. A few years later, in the late summer of 1963, his love of competition would set him down a path that would take him places far beyond their little house on Appleton.

"Bruh Boy, did you bring something to read from school today?" Mrs. Pittman asked, calling him by his family nickname. Charlie, who loved to read, had no reading assignments.

"No? Well, go get the newspaper, then," she said.

All of the Pittman kids knew the rules. After school, they had just a little time to play, and then their mother called them in to do their night's reading. If she asked, they had to discuss the day's schoolwork with her. If they had no schoolbooks, they had to read a newspaper or a magazine. Outside, the sounds of screeching children could still be heard as they played freeze tag, stickball, or just plain raced down the street. It seemed like the noise got louder—as if to taunt them—when they had to come in.

"Yes, ma'am," Charlie replied.

It was all he could do to stop from grinning as he read his newspaper. Charlie, as his friends called him, was a thin, raw-boned boy, tall for his age, with light eyes and big hands. He looked like he was moving even when he was standing still. On that day, the second day of football tryouts for Edmondson High School, Charlie officially became a football player! He ran faster than he ever had before to accomplish the feat, because on the first day of tryouts, he had missed the cut.

Anyone who knew him understood that meant he would move heaven and earth to make sure it didn't happen again. He couldn't resist a challenge.

His cash-strapped inner-city high school had a Darwinian method for selecting its players. Coach Augie Waibel only chose as many players as he had uniforms. The tryouts were without pads.

Seeing Charlie's evasive moves, which left defenders grabbing at air, he knew he had a keeper. "Get that boy a uniform!" he shouted to the equipment manager.

The Edmondson Redskins varsity never lost a game during Charlie's junior and senior years. At the end of his senior season, state high school officials presented him with a red and white football symbolizing his status as the Maryland high school football state scoring champion.

Yet football wasn't even his favorite sport. He liked football and basketball, but baseball was his love. He was a deadly infielder with quick hands, and his speed around the bases made each hit a headache for the opposing team.

Sure, Charlie could see the near horizon of his future; he'd get a job in the steel mills like his father and bring home $100 a week and raise his own family. But for right now, he could play ball almost all year long to his heart's content. And it did make him content.

Charlie lived for the challenges of sport; he played to win and he couldn't fathom the concept of playing not to lose. Football gave him answers to the questions that continually popped up in his mind: *Am I faster than that guy? Can I leap that trash can?* On the football field he learned the outer limits of his body's capabilities.

But it was on the baseball diamond that he learned what it meant to compete.

One summer, Charlie James went to see his son's all-black team play for the city championship against a white team. Young Charlie was playing first base when the white team's batter smashed a line drive between second and third bases. A critical double play was coming his way. A low throw from the shortstop squirted past his glove and the other team went on to win the state championship. After the game, his father called him over.

"Do you know why you lost that game?" his father asked.

"Because the shortstop threw the ball too low?" Charlie answered.

"No," his father replied. "You lost the game, Charles, because you missed the ball. 'The ball's too low' is an excuse, son. The ball can never get too low. You needed to field it."

From that day on, Charlie promised himself never to make excuses for his performances.

But it was Charlie's talents on the football field that were getting him noticed by a number of colleges. Though he expected to be working in a steel mill by the summer of 1966, suddenly he had opportunities to go to college. Notre Dame, Ohio State, Maryland, and Penn State were all interested in having him matriculate. They weren't alone in paying attention to him.

He was a legend at Edmondson: 35th out of 1,001 students academically; Parade Magazine High School All-American; Maryland Scoring Champion; High School Scholar-Athlete Award recipient, captain of the football team; and voted Most Likely to Succeed by his fellow students.

But it had all happened in the space of a few years. He still hadn't shaken the notion that he would be working in a steel mill in a year or two. And an aptitude test that he had taken and flunked worried him. Would he be able to cut it at a big college?

His English teacher, Mrs. Stella Gersek, tried to prepare him. Charlie was a special project for her, but not because of his athletic prowess. With classes full of teenagers who bragged loudly about their intimate knowledge of the street corners and seedy hangouts of west Baltimore, she knew Charlie and Rosalind were different. Even more, she was impressed by Jean Pittman's fierce protectiveness of her children. She knew the first-year English class was one of a college student's biggest challenges.

She took it upon herself to at least try and prepare Charlie for what to expect.

Adults were making it their business to get to know Charlie to "help" him, but he had no clue how this thing, this whole recruiting process, worked. His parents didn't know what to do about it, so they washed their hands of it and went about their lives; there was no one in the neighborhood he could go to and talk about it. With nowhere else to turn to when the recruiters came by, he asked his girlfriend Mauresé, who years later would become his wife, to help him with the strange etiquette and protocols of the fancy restaurants they took him to.

When it came time to choose a school, one of his athletic heroes, Lenny Moore, dominant as a running back at Penn State back in the '50s, played a factor in his final selection. He told Penn State coach Rip Engle he had narrowed his choice to Lou Saban's Maryland program or Penn State. Engle sent his running backs coach, George Welsh, to recruit Charlie, and Welsh returned with a verbal commitment from him.

But a short time later, Engle announced he was retiring after the 1965 season. He telephoned Charlie to break the news that a guy named Joe Paterno would be the new coach that fall.

Charlie wanted none of it.

"If I'm coming to Penn State," he said, "I'm playing for Rip Engle. I don't know anything about Joe Paterno. So I'm not coming."

After he got off the phone, he called Saban to tell him he would be attending Maryland.

Within minutes, Engle called back with Paterno on the line. Engle swore Paterno, an old quarterback, would be a great coach for him and that he'd create a stable program. Charlie remained unconvinced.

The next day, when he called Saban again to talk more about the situation, the Maryland coach made a fatal miscalculation.

Sensing that the deal was almost closed, Saban dangled a carrot in front of Charlie.

"You'll start at Maryland as a sophomore," Saban said. "If you go to Penn State, do you really think you'll be able to start as a sophomore?"

In that instant, Charlie knew where he had to go: Penn State. Saban had inadvertently painted his own program as second-rate.

When Charlie Pittman made the long car ride into Happy Valley, the nickname for State College, Pennsylvania, where Penn State is located, he felt as if he were slipping into a different dimension. The Nittany Mountains surrounded the bucolic campus and African American people—not just African American students— were hard to find. Less than one percent of the students were black. Worse still, on the football field, there were All-Americans and All-State athletes coming out of the woodwork.

Charlie roomed with Jim Kates of Plainfield, New Jersey. Kates was a linebacker, and the two were Paterno's first African American recruits. To have them tell it, it seemed they were the only black people on the 15,000-student campus.

Not everyone could handle such a profound change. Fred Rush, whom Charlie would meet years later in Erie, was a walk-on for the team. Rush, a gregarious young Pennsylvania native, was also black and would later joke that he went out for the football team to get girls but ran into a little problem.

"I was a decent player in high school," Rush recalls. "But I real-ized after I walked on at Penn State that you eventually have to get to crunch time—when the hitting starts. I swear I heard a coach tell some guy to hit me and break me into pieces. And the guy says, with this big, blank stare, 'Do you want me to hit him and break him into little pieces or big pieces?' He was serious! About that time, I decided to walk off."

Charlie had spent the summer running, in an effort to get a head start on his freshman year. He never lifted weights. The workout he devised for himself was devilishly simple. He would run a full-out 100-yard sprint and time himself. After running 10 or 15 of these sprints, his objective was to run at least one of the last sprints as fast as his best time. Tired and dripping sweat, he pushed himself to equal his fastest time. All the while, the words "fourth quarter" echoed in his mind.

He thought he was ready for anything, but when he walked onto the practice field for the first time, he heard a sound he'd never heard before—college-level hits in an empty stadium. These were hard, violent-sounding noises that rolled through the empty bleachers. If he was going to be spending time at the center of that cacophony, he wanted to have the proper equipment.

Being hit was not the problem; he just couldn't abide being lost in the shuffle. In the 1960s, college rules forbade freshmen from playing on varsity teams, so he was stuck with freshman coach Earl Bruce, dozens of other guys looking for a varsity spot the next year, and a whopping two games to showcase his skills. The right equipment was essential—he needed the perfect number for his jersey.

"When I first went out for the team, they gave me jersey No. 17," Pittman recalls. "I told the equipment manager that nobody great ever wore No. 17. I told him, 'I don't want it. I want a better number than that.' Lenny Moore was my idol and they gave me his number—No. 24. At the time, he was the greatest runner in Penn State history. Even though he wore 42 in college, he wore 24 as a pro. He wore spats; I wore spats. He was an NFL scoring champion; I was the Maryland scoring champion. I was very satisfied with that number."

Eighteen-year-old Charlie was set to create his destiny. But one more thing was needed. He would have to face the adversity most college athletes face—and it wasn't the realization that his competition vastly improved in the jump from high school. Bigger and stronger was a given; the winning edge at Penn State meant finding a way to excel in the classroom, too.

The classroom challenges that Mrs. Gersek had warned him about were even more arduous than he expected.

Luckily, his English professor was intrigued by him. Obviously intelligent, Charlie had a strange way of composing his assignments.

"You write exactly the way you talk," she said. His inner-city Baltimore accent placed him at a disadvantage in a writing composition class, so the instructor took it upon herself to tutor him. Occasionally, Mrs. Gersek would even write him to offer advice and encouragement.

Charlie also feared his speech class, Speech 200 by course name. In fact, he was too terrified to finish his first speech in front of his classmates. Again his instructor came to the rescue, allowing his first several speeches to be made in private.

"How can you play football in front of a crowd of thousands and then get flustered by a speech in front of a room of people?" the instructor teased.

Charlie was nearing his wits' end. Struggling with tough coursework, buried on the depth chart as a third-string running back, he confided in his roomate Jim Kates that it didn't seem fair. None of it.

As much as he grumbled, his legs still worked fine. In practice, he noticed he was outrunning and outperforming everyone else in the offensive backfield. For the benefit of Coach Bruce, on every practice play that he could he ran the ball into the end zone, for...illustrative purposes. Charlie was a raw ball carrier; he ran with two arms cradling the ball, resembling nothing so much as a speedy fireman rushing a baby out of a burning building.

One bright spot for him was that he was regularly called up to work with the varsity's scout team. His job was to run in a fashion similar to the star running back the varsity would face that week. He was able to spend time emulating Mel Farr of UCLA, Floyd Little of Syracuse, and Clint Jones of Michigan State.

Still, Coach Bruce was unmoved.

"Pittman, your stance is lousy!" he'd bark during freshman practice. It was too much for Charlie to bear.

One day after practice, he called his mother to tell her he'd made a huge mistake.

"Mom," he said. "This coach doesn't like me. I don't need this. I'm coming home."

Overhearing his wife's conversation, Charles Sr. picked up the line.

"You can leave there if you want, but you're not coming home," his father said. "Are those other boys quitting?"

"No, sir," Charlie said.

"You don't want to come back here and work in a steel mill, do you? You stay there."

Like many freshmen, Charlie was homesick. He missed his family, friends, and the familiar confines of Baltimore. He missed the playing time that allowed him to run in that top gear so few had.

After a freshman game in which he carried the ball two times for 14 yards, he was beginning to feel the weight of the world on his shoulder pads. After the game, he left the field in a pack of players, fans, coaches, and media. Helmet in hand, his head was hung low. In his mind, he knew the coaches would never notice this kind of output.

Then it came.

"Pittman!" Paterno shouted. "What kind of game did you have?"

"Just two carries...for 14 yards," he said sheepishly.

"When somebody asks you, you tell them you averaged seven yards a carry!" the coach replied.

Paterno—who was cultivating his reputation as a master motivator of young talent—may then have sensed Charlie's fragile confidence; he may have been sending a message to his star-to-be. Or maybe he just spoke louder than he intended. Whatever the reason, Charlie would forever remember overhearing what the young coach said to the man walking beside him.

"That's the guy who's going to make me a great football coach."

Charlie later found out the man to whom Paterno was speaking worked as an NFL scout. Between his father's insistence that he stay put and Paterno's praise, Charlie had found his way again. He had made his last call asking if he could come home.

Paterno was an Ivy League–educated hustler. He inherited a stable program that produced the occasional Lenny Moore or Roosevelt Grier as stars and usually won between five and seven games a year. Rip Engle saw Joe as a good guy, a Brooklyn kid who was loyal as the day was long. He brought him in from Brown University in 1950. It might have been Engle's intent to make a regional power out of Penn State. And he might have thought his friend was of the same mind when he recommended him for the head coach's job. But Paterno had a bigger vision. And he knew how to use sportswriters to his advantage.

Paterno began tirelessly floating the notion of Penn State as a national power to anyone with a pen and notepad.

"What if we had the best of both worlds?" urged Paterno's carnie patter, drawing attention by asking a question. "What if Penn State kids were smart enough to graduate from Harvard and athletic enough to beat Alabama?"

Any reporter who could tell an I formation from a wing T was hooked. That type of player didn't exist in nature, and they wanted to hear more.

Paterno then tied it up with a ribbon for them; he called it a Grand Experiment.

One can almost hear the reporter's response upon hearing about this crazy chimera.

"Go on…"

By 1966, America was in turmoil. War raged in Southeast Asia. President John F. Kennedy and Malcolm X were three and two years in the grave, respectively. Dr. Martin Luther King Jr. had less than two years to live and music and drugs had merged into some smoky amalgam that adults feared would rot their children's minds.

Confidence, America's stock-in-trade, was taking a beating with each assassination, with each new drug, with every living room

TV's broadcast of coffins returning from Vietnam. It was easy to be scared; it was a reasonable reaction. Black or white, young or old, the 1960s were a turbulent time for all—and it was Charlie's coming of age. He needed all the confidence he could find.

So much innocence had been lost by 1966 that even America's dream industry of feature films began to trumpet bad boys and girls as antiheroes—*Bonnie and Clyde*, *The Wild Bunch*, and *Butch Cassidy and the Sundance Kid* were the new prototypes—and everybody died in the end.

But a boy and his football? Life could be pure again, with the right boy, the right parents, the right dream, and the right coach.

Even if the time wasn't right.

Before he ever stepped onto the turf at Beaver Stadium, Charlie Pittman was being readied for the Paterno Era and Penn State by Charlie James and Jean Pittman, who were less interested in a Grand Experiment than a Grand Existence for their own "team." Discipline, planning, and respect were nonnegotiable if they wanted to make that happen.

Charlie couldn't come home because coming home meant giving up.

Had he turned his back on Penn State, Charlie would have returned to a community beginning to crack: unwed mothers, marijuana smokers, and a white police force that had begun to exhibit more brutal behavior toward young men of color.

"I survived it by keeping myself motivated," Charlie recalls, more than 40 years removed from those days. "One of my primary motivations was to succeed and do well. I was picked as most likely to succeed in high school and I've always taken that pretty seriously. Much of my success is due to a fear of failure. Never losing football games becomes a great motivator. I learned to always play to win instead of playing not to lose. There are always people looking to protect themselves because they are playing not to lose. Those situations make me want to exceed what I think I can do."

Down to Business Charlie Pittman may have been a very young man, but two of his action choices in the above passages showed a maturity well beyond his age. His first action was to choose Penn State based on Saban's comments; the second was to choose his jersey number.

How does an 18-year-old possess the savvy to hear what a recruiter is really saying? In the course of turning down Maryland, Charlie did something amazing that you should do in your career. He listened to what was being said to him, instead of hearing what he wanted to hear.

When Coach Saban told him he was basically guaranteed to play as a sophomore at Maryland, he wanted Charlie to hear: "We will play you sooner than Penn State will play you."

Charlie heard what he was really saying: "You're good, but not good enough to start as a sophomore in that program. Here at Maryland, on the other hand…"

Was the youngster's astute interpretation a result of learned behavior or sophistication brought on by being subjected to intense recruiting visits? Doesn't matter. Make that habit part of your nature and nurture it. Listen to the talk in your office; listen to friends, foes, and acquaintances and translate all of it as if it were a foreign language. Every day of your life people are saying things to you that you're not hearing.

Secondly, recognize the greatness inside you. Charlie recognized his own greatness; let that be your template. You might argue that he had an advantage in that regard. You might note that for a three-year period he was the object of cheers, pep rallies, glowing newspaper articles, swooning girls, recruiting visits, and accolades that would swell the head of

Mahatma Gandhi—and you'd be right. But prior to that short period of time, he was considered a geeky kid who had to be in the house before the street lamps came on. Before the sudden glory, he was anticipating a very pedestrian future as a steelworker.

But a switch was flipped inside him. That switch exists inside all of us.

By the time fate had brought him to the equipment manager's room in the bowels of Beaver Stadium, he knew a champion had to recognize he was a champion. For Charlie, being a champion meant donning Lenny Moore's magic No. 24. For the late senator Paul Simon it meant wearing a bow tie; for billionaire Donald Trump it means avoiding handshakes and naming everything Trump.

Find your own No. 24. That probably doesn't mean that you stencil a big "2" and "4" on the back of your business suit, but rather that you consciously choose—a very powerful action—the outward manifestation of your style. In the early 1990s, the rap duo Kriss Kross gained a measure of fame for wearing their clothes backward. Where is your comfort zone?

Will you choose a color like Johnny Cash, the Man in Black? Or will you wear a ponytail like music superproducer Jimmy "Jam" Harris?

Now that you've dedicated yourself to "listening" and not "hearing" and you're close to selecting your personal victory totem, it is time to listen.

Next Generation

Tony Pittman was the first child born to Charles and Mauresé Pittman, childhood sweethearts who have been married since

1970. By the time of Tony's birth, his father was finishing his two-year stint in the NFL. His two sisters, Mauresa and Kira, were born shortly after, and the three were an inseparable band in the Pittman household.

Tony was a compact child with a shy streak when he was very young. He loved to quietly explore, whether it was the family's spacious house in Erie, Pennsylvania, where his father worked for Marine Bank, or the nearby woods.

Charles Pittman would pull Tony's talents to the surface whenever possible. He'd challenge his son mentally and physically. How fast can you run? Can you count to 10?

"Yes," Tony would reply.

Each time Charles would say, "Show me."

When Tony was three, his father rushed into the house in Erie. He had attended a Pittsburgh Steelers game with a friend who had been bragging on the car ride about his own three-year-old, who could count to 100.

"Come on, Tony," his father said, picking him up and carrying him off. "We're going to learn to count to 100."

Tony enjoyed the attention from his father. He would catch his father's excitement as Charles taught him to tell time using a paper plate. He preferred trying to puzzle out the world by himself. But if the answers didn't come, Mom and Dad would solve the mystery for him. He used that as a last resort. He loved finding his own way.

Even as a child he needed a little solitude and a calm mind to solve the world's mysteries. Wherever he traveled, to the backyard or the school grounds, he would find a moment to absorb his surroundings—taking in the sights, the sounds—remembering, then analyzing. In grade school, for instance, his father coached his soccer team, and Tony noticed that his dad talked to some of his teammates differently than others.

He'd pull some kids aside and talk to them privately. Others he would praise in front of the group. It brought to mind Tony's favorite question.

"Why?"

Tony drove his parents to distraction with that question. His father tried to explain that different kids needed to be motivated— Tony grappled with the adult word—differently than other kids. Motivated. He would have to remember that word. It seemed important.

Tony was a preschooler the day he came across his father acting strangely. The youngster had seen his dad set the telephone down and put his head in his hands, something he had never seen his dad do.

"Why are you crying?"

Tony's father, who would answer six or seven of Tony's questions in a row on most days, had no answer for him.

He would find a way to explain later, but he didn't have the words at that moment to say his sister Rosalind, Tony's favorite aunt, was dead. Twenty-nine years old, funny, fiercely intelligent, and unbent by a life that dulled her dreams simply because she was a woman—she was gone.

Her husband had stabbed her to death in a crime of passion.

Always a close family, Mauresé and Charles seemed to huddle even closer with Tony after Rosalind's funeral.

The Pittmans, saddened by the bright potential that Rosalind's death cut short, dug in to prepare their son for a successful future. It had been a hard 12-month period—10 months earlier, another tragedy had struck when Charlie James Pittman, Charles's father, died of colon cancer at the age of 53.

Charles was hit hard by the loss of his sister and father. His father had been a steadying presence. In that deep voice of his, he could have pronounced running "foolishness" and stopped Charles more surely than any tackler, but he never did.

"Charlie's father was a great man," remembers Paterno. "I remember when I had him over to my house on a recruiting visit, and he hung back. I walked over to him and asked him to join the group, but he wanted to make sure Charlie had his day."

And Rosalind. Her academic brilliance was the star her brothers pursued but could never catch. Her future should have been brighter. Now his mother had an empty house, but she'd never be alone. Charles vowed that both of his families—the family he'd grown up with and the family he'd made—would do well.

In a few years, Tony would attend McDowell High School on West 38th Street in Erie. In a foreshadowing of his football future, the McDowell Trojans had team colors of blue and white, and their archrival was Cathedral Preparatory School, whose team wore gold helmets à la Notre Dame. The schools were bitter enemies on the football field. But classrooms were just a part of Tony's education. Charles took it upon himself to test Tony's character.

"I felt like I had to teach him to handle defeat," Charles recalls. "He was kind of a shy and bashful kid, and shy, bashful kids can take to those lessons pretty slowly."

Charles decided to teach Tony about defeat by first inoculating him against it. His son would be a winner.

"I wouldn't let Tony play football until he was in ninth grade," he recalls. "I didn't want him to lose at that early age. So I let him get a taste of winning for his confidence.

"It's strange, but people handle defeat better than they do success. I was determined that that was not going to be the case for my son or daughters. Tony got his early competition from soccer, basketball, and piano lessons—never football. My friends would tell me that if I didn't get him on the football field soon, he'd be behind. I said, 'No. I want him to get physically stronger and acquire his mental toughness.' He had to get to a place where he honestly believed he could compete at a very high level and beat bigger and stronger kids. Winning is a habit, just as much as losing is a habit."

Tony, who had been waiting for the day when he could play football, finally saw that day come. By his 10th-grade year, he was a good enough offensive player that he earned a trophy: Joe Paterno, his father's old coach and good friend, sent him a letter.

"I still have his letter framed in my house," Tony says. "Joe wrote me in the fall of 1986, right before they won the national championship against Miami. I was in 10th grade and had just started playing football. Joe wrote me and said, 'We've got our eye on you.'"

At the time, Tony stood about 5'8" and weighed 165 pounds. He was a flash on the field and wiry from lifting weights.

Still, Tony needed some seasoning. Despite his father's work on his mental toughness, competing at an elite level would be difficult for someone with his slight build. There was no doubt that Tony wanted to play college sports. Charles knew Tony had two things in his favor: one was physical and one was mental.

Tony's physical gift was that he was a bolt of lightning in a footrace; it was a different, more compact gait than Charles had possessed as a young man, but it ate up the turf just as fast. Tony's mental talent was his perserverance.

"If Tony came across a problem he didn't know the answer to," Charles said, "he was a bulldog until he figured it out. I don't care how long it took."

"The bulldog" had set his sights on a college athletic career.

Charles and Mauresé obliged him and made one of the most difficult decisions of their marriage so that Tony could pursue his dream. They sent him away to Phillips Academy in Andover, Massachusetts, for two years. In effect, Tony added a year to his high school career in hopes of maturing enough to play big-time college football. The cost of the move—tuition was about $22,000 per year—affected the family's finances, but that was secondary to the burden on Charles and Mauresé's hearts.

Charles loved to come home and play catch or go walking with his eldest child. Tony's intent observations of the world around him sometimes surprised his father.

"He's a very deep thinker," Charles noted of his son on more than one occasion.

If Charles knew what Tony was thinking as he began what would eventually be a seven-year journey to match his father's undefeated season, he would have been doubly proud.

I'm going to start at Penn State, and I'm going to wear No. 24, Tony thought.

Tony graduated with honors from Penn State. He earned a bachelor of science degree in industrial engineering, as well as an MBA from the school. In the business world he's worked in the consulting, IT, and supply chain fields. Currently with EDS (Electronic Data Systems), he previously worked for IBM in its Integrated Supply Chain division. Prior to that he worked for several firms, including PricewaterhouseCoopers and what is now BearingPoint.

His career is a testament to being able to adapt in a radically changing business climate. His position titles have included technical consultant, database administrator, and supply chain integrations manager.

Tony's face is the face of the 21st-century global employee: he is tech-savvy, self-contained, adaptable, and attractive to employers because he is extremely well educated. What would have been catastrophic to the workers of previous generations—an industry shakeout or a failed company—he is able to take in stride. Though he hasn't lost a job, he doesn't fear the prospect. The answer, he says, lies in teamwork.

"I'm never going to assume the current global economy will ever revert to how it was when my father was starting his career," he says. "Kids today enter the workforce expecting to have four or five or six jobs in their career, not one job for life. Companies that don't get that are probably operating under a false sense of security. They're going to see the impact of an economy that they won't be ready for.

"I'm certainly not going to eyeball one company for life. And they're not going to stick with me if I maintain only one set of skills for life. I have a friend who is a surgeon and I tell him that, out of all of us, he's the one that's set. The need for what he does probably won't change very much. Look at me. Six years ago, when I could sit down and crank out line after line of code, I was in high demand for that skill set. Today, that kind of work goes to China or India. I loved programming; it made me happy when I knew I was going to sit in a room and write code all day. But I also knew that merry-go-round was never going to get me anywhere. The signs were there that programming was becoming a commodity skill.

"Fast forward five or six years to the present and that, indeed, came to pass. I think the real issue for today's workforce is how to handle a new reality, this shifting economy.

"I strongly believe you cannot overcome the negatives without having a true team mentality—not when commitment is rarely given by employers or employees. The old paradigms don't work. Companies can't promise jobs that will never go away and stock the buildings with people who have little incentive other than collecting paychecks. People aren't commodities. There's a different type of Darwinism at play in the workplace today that tells the survivors, 'You better not be afraid of change; you better not be afraid to move.' There is no core characteristic for successful workers other than they need to be agile and adaptable. There is no sustainable advantage for either companies or industries in the new economy.

"Teamwork can help mitigate that. A team is a collection of people with diverse skills who come together for a period of time. Based on everything I've seen, the future will belong to companies that understand and play up teamwork to succeed."

One of the most important things a successful team does is anticipate adversity and manage it. That's a lesson for the next chapter.

WINNING IN LIFE

"No. 17? Nobody great ever wore No. 17. I don't want it. I want a better number than that."

—*Charles Pittman*

CHAPTER 2

Managing Adversity

O n October 1, 1994, the Nittany Lions weren't having a tough time with the Temple Owls football team. Even on Temple's home turf, Franklin Field, the Lions were rolling to an eventual 48–21 rout. Owls head coach Ron Dickerson had been Tony Pittman's position coach at Penn State before leaving for Clemson, then taking the top spot at Temple. Dickerson was a good coach, but the talent wasn't there for him. Still, it was clear Dickerson had the Owls geared up for State. By the second quarter, Tony (playing corner-back, covering the receiver who ran the deep pattern) had had enough abuse. As he had done all game, the guy was talking trash as he ran. With no chance to win, his trash-talking makes no sense, Tony thought. Well-versed in the nuances of competition from early childhood, Tony knew the guy was gearing himself up to do some-thing stupid. In a preemptive strike, Tony hit him, knocking him to the ground. Tony stood over the stunned player as the yellow flags flew. It took getting a penalty, but the trash-talking stopped.

Adversity is the name of the game for big-time college football players. Adversity exists at the core of any competition. Competition, after all, is a situation in which one participant has something the other competitor wants—and opposes giving it away. Like business, football filters out most of the people who want to play at the highest levels. Some don't have the physical skills, some lack mental toughness, some are too easily injured, some are in the wrong place at the wrong time. Or combinations of the above may apply.

Joe Paterno understands the need to filter out most players. In fact, his Grand Experiment, which was to recruit serious scholars who could handle college-level education then choose the best athletes from that number, caught the attention of the sports world precisely because he was setting up such a stringent talent filter for his program.

For Paterno, it just made sense to recruit intelligent athletes.

"We were going through a period [in this country] where football players had to be real tough, mean guys," Paterno recalls. "In the classroom, people were making excuses for them. But I played football at an Ivy League school and some of the brightest guys at the university were on that team. I thought we could be a good football team and have people who could take advantage of the athletic and educational opportunities—and then go on and do something significant in the larger community, like Charlie and Tony."

Forty-odd years later, what was once considered folly is now a source of pride. It's a Penn State tradition among the former football players to discuss which physically gifted high school recruits won't get a call from Paterno—because they're not Penn State material.

Yet even with its emphasis on education, the Penn State tradition turns out some of the best football players in the world—Paterno's program has sent more than 200 to the NFL—and adversity is the crucible that forms those players. But exposure to adversity is just one side of Paterno's successful equation. The other is to build up confidence—in the program and in one's own abilities. More specifically, a positive self-confidence has to be nurtured, according to Paterno, and it should never overshadow the team.

Charlie Pittman's confidence grew exponentially after Paterno complimented him, via stage whisper, during his freshman year. At the dawn of his sophomore season, he called back home and bragged to his mother that he would be starting by the third game of the season.

"Watch," he said. "When we play UCLA, I'll be starting."

That would have been news to Paterno. Bobby Campbell wore the blue jersey. A blue jersey meant, like every other starter, he was number one on the depth chart. Paterno's game plan called for Campbell to anchor the halfback spot for all of 1967. Campbell led the 1966 team in rushing and he was set for an even better 1967 season. Charlie, on the other hand, wore a yellow practice jersey—a step down from even the green jerseys of the second stringers.

Charlie didn't care. Paterno's carefully laid depth charts were irrelevant. He had spent his short career fighting for the right to don football jerseys. He spent his youth running down the fastest kids on the sandlots until all of them fell behind him. Sure, there were more people watching and it was more highly organized, but in Charlie's mind it was the sandlots of Baltimore all over again. This time he was chasing down Bobby Campbell, who was holding a blue jersey that Charlie intended to take away.

The first two games of the season it looked as if Campbell and that blue jersey were beyond Charlie's reach. In a 23–22 season-opening loss to Navy and a 17–8 win over Miami (FL), Campbell performed magnificently. He rushed for more than 100 yards in each game with a ridiculously high 6.9 average yards per rushing attempt.

Against Navy, Charlie, who had suffered a painful hip pointer in practice, started the second half of the game and shared the backfield with Campbell, but he never touched the ball.

It was humiliating. There he was in his home state with friends and family rooting for him and he was a glorified placeholder. After leaving the locker room, he called on his mother and apologized for the game—and one more thing.

"I'm sorry I made that prediction," he said. "I don't know if I'm going to start."

Starting became an issue for several of the seniors on the team as well. Paterno saw the loss against Navy, a soft team in his eyes, as an indictment against his own defense. Half-hearted efforts from his players irritated Paterno and he felt slapped in the face by the performance of several of his seniors. After the Navy game, he benched eight seniors, redesigned the defense, and started playing sophomores.

He vividly remembers making that change.

"The first 11 games I coached, we were 5–6," Paterno recalls. "We had some guys who were hotshot players, who had been big names in high school. But I felt we had some guys on the bench that I thought were better players. I figured we're not going anywhere with these other guys, so it made sense to me to give those young guys some playing time."

Even with Paterno's move to use more underclassmen, the game against Miami proved to be no better for Charlie. Campbell had the spot he coveted locked down. Charlie shuttled in and out, but Paterno called no plays for him.

By the time the UCLA game rolled around, Charlie knew he wouldn't be starting. And that was a pity because the UCLA contest meant that a flood of sportswriters would descend on Happy Valley. It would have been a great coming-out party.

The oddly named university, the University of California, Los Angeles (UCLA), was the hottest sports story of the year. It was the defending national champion in college basketball with a junior center named Lew Alcindor and they fielded the fourth-ranked football team in the nation. The football Bruins featured eventual 1967 Heisman Trophy winner Gary Beban at quarterback and were helmed by crafty coach Tommy Prothro. Critics accused Prothro of cheating—going high-tech before there was high-tech—by wiring a radio receiver in Beban's helmet in its 1966 blowout against Penn State.

The Bruins even had an attention-grabbing rivalry. UCLA's cross-town neighbor, the University of Southern California, had an electric running back by the name of Orenthal James "O.J." Simpson, who was shattering USC rushing records and pushing Beban for the Heisman.

Though the Bruins destroyed Penn State in 1966 by a score of 49–11, Paterno had the press believing in his young team and his starting halfback.

The game proved to be a treat for football fans—two tough teams knocked heads to see who would be the last one standing. Campbell scored the first points of that game on a three-yard sweep. After the PAT made it 7–0, Paterno unleashed his defensive dogs on Beban. Upperclassmen Jim Litterelle and Frank Spaziani, along with sophomore Steve Smear, took turns hounding Beban with 10 blitzes for negative 45 yards. Penn State held that 7–0 lead for the entire first half.

It was an amazing start for the unranked Nittany Lions, but it came at a cost. Campbell seriously injured his knee and couldn't report for the second half.

"Pittman, you're starting the second half for Bobby," Paterno barked.

With those eight words, Paterno had again ratcheted up his young back's confidence. Charlie wasn't a starter, but he would be the main back for the second half. His prediction for his mother had been close—just off by half a game. Charlie didn't score any points or break for a long run, but he was a solid presence, avoiding fumbles with that two-handed carrying style of his, pushing for extra yards and always in the right place.

UCLA, however, had gained momentum. The Bruins kicked a 37-yard field goal to close the gap to 7–3, and then scored 10 unanswered points by recovering a Lions' fumble and blocking a punt. Penn State's Tom Cherry scored late in the game on a two-yard touchdown run and a two-point conversion. At game's end, UCLA had escaped Beaver Stadium with a 17–15 win.

Charlie earned his first-ever start in the next game against Boston College. He and fellow sophomores Peter Johnson, Neal Smith, Steve Smear, Jim Kates, and Dennis Onkotz began playing regularly and something special was brewing. Sportswriters dubbed the light, fast State backfield the Rover Boys.

On October 14, 1967, the Lions took to the field against Boston College and the revamped defense was stalwart. Once again, Charlie was solid but uninspiring in the offensive backfield. Penn State thumped Boston College 50–28, but Paterno wasn't through tinkering with his young team yet.

Paterno incorrectly believed Charlie's two-handed carrying style meant he was switching the football from hand to hand.

"Charlie would run with the ball in one arm and then switch it to the other. I guess he was trying to keep it away from where it could be knocked out of his hands," Paterno recalls. "I thought that was just a fumble waiting to happen."

At the next practice, Paterno made a point of seeking Charlie out.

"Can you run the football without switching hands?" Paterno asked.

At first he was confused, but quickly understood his coach wanted him to run the ball with one arm or the other.

"I'll give it a try," Charlie said.

Charlie earned his second start on homecoming at Beaver Stadium against the West Virginia Mountaineers on October 21, 1967. After Paterno questioned his ball carrying, Charlie lived with a football under one arm. For the week leading up to the game, he ran with his left arm free and a football tucked into his right armpit. He allowed the ball to be slapped at, punched, and clawed until he felt comfortable that it was going nowhere during a real game. In fact, it stayed put for most of his college career. Charlie fumbled three times in college—and two of them happened in his sophomore year. The final fumble came in his junior year.

Paterno had tapped him to receive the second-half kickoff. One-handed Charlie took the kickoff and flew downfield as if he were again fighting for a jersey at Edmondson High. The Mountaineers' defense couldn't touch him. Eighty-three yards later, he was in the end zone and the Lions were up by a touchdown. By game's end, Charlie had finished with 265 all-purpose yards, a Penn State sophomore record that still stood in 2007. Penn State won 21–14, but could have scored more.

Sly as ever, Paterno didn't want to show his hand to the Syracuse scouts: scouts for the team they were playing the following week. Colleges scout the games of upcoming opponents to help create a game plan. For instance, if a team has a great run defense, scouts might suggest more passing offense. Syracuse featured a bruising back named Larry Csonka who would cause enough problems without the Lions laying bare their offensive schemes.

The two-game winning streak seemed to be a double-secret signal for Paterno and his staff to work the Lions players to within an inch of their lives. Charlie's two starts brought to mind an old saying for him—"Be careful what you wish for." He was a starter, but his workload had risen astronomically. Starters took hits in practice that rang bells in their helmets. Missed assignments brought howls of protest from coaching staff. Sweat, pain, and verbal abuse were the rewards for being young, athletic, and winners of two games in a row.

On the Tuesday before the Syracuse game, Penn State linebackers coach Dan "Bad Rad" Radakovich stepped gingerly around the big blue *S* in the carpet of the locker room. Stepping on the *S* meant an immediate 30 push-ups for anyone, even coaches, and Bad Rad was looking for a victim, not exercise. It was his Tuesday routine.

Don't come by here—go mess with someone else! Charlie thought as he put on his uniform in front of his locker. The assistant coach had an evil smile on his face. Charlie tried to hurry and get dressed before he made it over.

"Pittman!"

"Yes, sir?"

"Are you ready to bleed? Because the linebackers can't wait to give you your beating!"

I know, Charlie thought. *They're not happy unless you're bleeding.*

Charlie dreaded Tuesdays of game weeks. "Bloody Tuesdays," groaning teammates called them. The coaches ran a variety of drills and most were pretty simple. One was to put a linebacker and a running back in front of each other, give the running back the ball and order him to run five yards ahead. The space was always so narrow it was pointless to try to put a move on the defensive guy. It was a test of testicular fortitude—go straight ahead and, like Bad Rad said, take your beating.

Complaining to running backs coach George Welsh made no difference—in fact, whining about it usually made the hits a little stiffer.

"But the absolute worst thing to hear in practice was when Joe said 'Let's go, blue on blue,'" Charles recalls. "That meant the offensive starters had a live scrimmage against the defensive starters. When Joe had us go blue on blue, I'd buckle up my chinstrap and make sure I kept my eye on John Ebersole and Mike Reid."

Campbell returned to practice after the West Virginia game ready to pick up where he left off. He and Charlie sat in the film room and studied the Syracuse defense, ran through the drills. Each was aware of the events of recent weeks; each was certain he was the number one back—and both noticed the other's blue jersey. It would only be sorted out when the team ran its offensive sets for the week.

"Blue! Get in the huddle!" Paterno said at last. Charlie and Campbell both ran to the huddle.

Years later, Pittman recalled that moment.

"I'm standing in the huddle, he's standing in the huddle. I'm not going to tell him to get out and he's sure not going to tell me to get out."

"Bobby!" Paterno bellowed. "Get out of the huddle! You've got to earn your spot back!"

"Man!" Pittman recalls. "That was such a vote of confidence for me!"

The Syracuse game showed Paterno how tough his confident young tailback was; Charlie scored the first touchdown of the game and kept a brutal Orange defense honest with a couple dozen gutsy rushes. Two-hundred and thirty-pound Csonka, as Paterno expected, was wearing down his defenders. Syracuse coach Ben Schwartzwalder put the ball in his hands and received 32 carries for 115 yards and two touchdowns from his fullback. Penn State quarterback Tom Sherman countered Csonka's ground game with a 60-yard touchdown strike to talented tight end Ted Kwalick and a quarterback sneak from the one-yard line. The Lions led at the half by a score of 22–14. But Csonka's second touchdown made it 22–20 as the game clock wound down. The Lions couldn't put any points on the board on their next series of possessions and had to punt—leaving the Orange just a field goal away from a win.

But with 1:07 to go, one of the Rover Boys, Onkotz, picked off a pass by Syracuse quarterback Rick Cassata and ran it back 53 yards for the 29–20 final score.

Charlie was proving to be a reliable back. He would finish out the season with 580 yards rushing, 4.9 yards per carry rushing average, seven touchdowns, and a second-place finish in total points for the Lions with 42.

By the time the Lions played coach Lou Saban's Maryland Terrapins—the team that Charlie almost joined—they were a totally different group. In 1966, Penn State had squeaked out a 15–7 victory over Maryland. But the 1967 matchup borrowed from longtime Houston Oilers' coach Bum Phillips's book of quotations: "Last year we knocked on the door. This year, we kicked the son of a gun in." Charlie ran at will against the Terrapins in a 38–3 victory that saw him rest for most of the fourth quarter.

With his starting spot safe, Charlie and the new-look Nittany Lions were confident. They had a four-game winning streak and were ready to make hay. Oddsmakers were more inclined to believe they were going to make fools of themselves against their next opponent, North Carolina State. Led by linebacker and team captain Chuck Amato, the Wolfpack defenders were called the

White Shoes gang and they were absolutely feared by opponents. Teams couldn't run or pass against them and the 'Pack had strolled through their schedule with shocking ease. Years later, Amato would speak words that applied to him and his fellow Wolfpack defenders in 1967: "We want to chase the football hard, and we want to get there with a bad disposition."

When Pittsburgh-based TV sports reporter Lou Prato covered that game, he knew he was seeing the start of something amazing all those years ago.

Prato stretched and breathed in the acrid smell of popcorn and something he fervently hoped was the aroma of hot dogs. The Channel 11-Pittsburgh TV news reporter stood in the drafty confines of Beaver Stadium spending another Saturday in 1967 covering his beloved Nittany Lions. The award-winning journalist was in the press box of the venerable old stadium, but this time he was not working for a newspaper. No, Prato was covering Penn State football in front of a television camera. He had to smile to himself because it hadn't been easy to get back into the stadium's nosebleed section with the great view of Mt. Nittany. Prato had to twist the arm of his producer Dave Kelly to convince Kelly that sleepy Penn State would be a draw for fickle TV football fans. To his credit, Kelly recognized that he could draw an audience the station hadn't been reaching. Pittsburgh was Pitt Panthers territory and Nittany Lions fans had been second-class viewers. A few thousand more viewers would translate into a few more advertising dollars. Prato wasn't concerned about the financial calculations of the decision; he was a fan of the team.

Prato, a 1959 graduate of Penn State, would later become the director of the Penn State All-Sports Museum. In 1998, he would publish the definitive bible for Penn State football—*The Penn State Football Encyclopedia*. The Saturday saga unfolding on November 11, 1967, would hold an honored place in the encyclopedia.

On that glorious fall day he looked down on the field at one of his favorite players, Charlie Pittman, who was bareheaded, sweaty, and anxiously surveying the action against North Carolina State.

The lanky Pittman had had another strong game. These young Lions were the talk of the nation. A tough defense and Pittman's mad dashes were part of the reason for the attention. Pittman, his roommate Jim Kates, Pete Johnson, Neal Smith, Steve Smear, and Dennis Onkotz were the strong who so impressed followers of the sport. Heisman Trophy rumblings were already beginning for the callow Baltimore native, who had stepped up when sensational tailback Bobby Campbell had gone down with a knee injury. Second-year coach Joe Paterno would have liked to accept the sportswriters' bestowing their mantle of genius by saying he knew all along these young guys were ready for the big time. But he was too honest for that ruse. With a shrug and a pair of upturned palms he told reporters the truth. Injuries, mediocre play by his seniors, and graduation had his team snake bitten. He pinned his hopes on 10 green sophomores—the Super Sophomores—because there was no other alternative.

Every early season press conference saw Paterno pulling out his thick black hair fretting about his inexperienced defense. In the opening season loss to coach Bill Elias's Navy team, the Midshipmen ran amok with 564 yards in total offense. That was an amazing amount of productivity for a so-so college football team—and Paterno's reason for benching his senior defenders.

Paterno was no fool. When analyzing that game, he noticed his own team had gained 621 yards against Navy; his backfield showed real talent and toughness. Now, four games later, he saw exactly how much talent. If he was forced to unleash his Super Sophomores, then Charlie for one could not have been happier.

Charlie, whom national sports writers said could gain a yard against the Empire State Building, still had fans buzzing about his 83-yard kickoff return against West Virginia. Penn State was averaging a torrid 34.5 points a game during its winning streak.

But in the closing seconds of the North Carolina State game, it was no longer up to Pittman and the young offense. Penn State starters had been held to 13 points by the veteran White Shoes gang.

Pittman's early game rushes gave the Lions good field position, if not points. The North Carolina State defense was swarming and Penn State, despite the speed of Charlie and his brethren, were hitting a defensive wall against the more experienced Wolfpack and its 17 seniors.

Luckily, the Lions had a cushion. They scored 13 points quickly in the first quarter on two spectacular plays—an 18-yard pass to tight end Kwalick and a 67-yard interception and return by linebacker Onkotz. After those scores, the team was stifled. Three times a combination of Charlie's runs and quarterback Tom Sherman's passes got the Lions into the red zone—within 20 yards of the goal. Being that close to a touchdown generally makes offenses salivate. But in three tries, Penn State came up empty.

In the meantime, a determined North Carolina State was patiently scoring two field goals, narrowing the gap to 13–6 as the fourth quarter began.

The fourth quarter is where legends are made, and Penn State possessed no real legendary games in its history. But it had one by the tail on that Saturday.

Third-ranked North Carolina State was undefeated after eight games. It had a Hall of Fame–caliber coach in Earle Edwards, and the team would end the season with a 9-2 record and a 14–7 Liberty Bowl victory over powerhouse Georgia. A year later, they would be Atlantic Coast Conference co-champions. But that day, the Lions were facing a tough, talented, motivated, and more experienced opponent.

"It was 13–6 in the fourth," Prato remembers. "In my mind, it was a defining moment for the program. North Carolina State was a tough team and it was well-coached by Earle Edwards—an old Penn State guy."

Forty seconds remained in the game. North Carolina State had the ball and a fourth down on the Lions' 1-yard line. It was time to either make history or break hearts.

The play the Lions' defense anticipated was one they had been seeing all afternoon. Wolfpack halfback Tony Barchuk, who had 93 yards on 28 carries, was going up the middle. Fans in Beaver Stadium knew, viewers of Prato's broadcast knew, Kalahari Bushmen probably knew: Barchuk would get the ball.

As the linemen for the two teams thunderclapped together for the crucial play, Onkotz took split-second notice of the Wolfpack line blocking toward the middle. He rushed to help jam it. Barchuk saw the pileup and knew he had one chance: hurdle the line.

Onkotz met him in a jarring collision a foot from the goal line and five feet in the air. Barchuk ended up on his back…two yards short of a touchdown.

Pittman and every able body on the Lions' sideline leapt skyward.

The game ended with a safety tallied by North Carolina State for a 13–8 final score. Five wins in a row and all of a sudden these young men, this team, was something special.

"Those were some great teams," *Centre Daily Times* editor Ron Bracken says. "It's interesting that it worked out the way it did for Charlie and Tony. They played on some of the greatest teams Paterno ever had. In 1968, 1969 Penn State hadn't reached the level that it had when Tony got there. But those 1968 and 1969 teams are always going to be special. They were the program's first undefeated teams. It's remarkable that those teams, Charlie's teams, were noted more for defense than offense; and Tony played defense on a team that will forever be known for its offense. Both of them were in the shadow of the other unit. [Still,] they feel they are good enough to do whatever it takes to meet a challenge. They can handle it. Courage, I guess you could call it."

In August 1990, Tony Pittman recognized some of the new guys on the turf practice fields of Holuba Hall; he'd read their press clippings. Over there was the big tight end, Kyle Brady, quarterbacks Kerry Collins and John Sacca were tossing footballs a few yards away, and linebacker Phil Yeboah-Kodie was stretching in the late-afternoon sun. Many were freshmen like Tony. Others had made their names playing for Penn State the year before—wide receiver O.J. McDuffie, John Sacca's brother, Tony Sacca, and tailback Leroy Thompson were back for the 1990 season.

"My first practice. I remember I got there a week early. We all kind of knew each other by name, but you really don't know what a guy can do from the press clippings," Tony recalls. "We didn't even know what position we were going to play. It was like we were a science experiment. Joe has a reputation for saying where you'll play. At one point, he was going to play [then high school quarterback] Jim Kelly as a linebacker."

Kelly, a Pennsylvania kid, of course went to the University of Miami, where he set dozens of passing records as a quarterback, before going pro in the fabled Quarterback Class of 1983. Kelly is in the Pro Football Hall of Fame.

"Joe put you where he thought you belonged," Tony says. "There were a lot of guys who didn't know where they were going to end up."

No matter where they ended up, football players at Penn State knew they would have to get past the tough spring practice stretch each year before seeing light at the end of the tunnel. Elite football players have a love-hate relationship with the month of April.

"Oh, man. April is hard," Tony says. "Spring practice; there are no crowds and you have to do all the work anyway. Other kids, your friends, are relaxing, sunbathing; the weather's nice and there you are: having to hit in full pads. Spring practices are among the toughest things I've ever done. They might say otherwise, but the coaches don't have to preserve your body, so they're really putting you through your paces. Mentally, it is tough to get in the right frame of mind."

Some might argue that Tony's entire football career was a never-ending April—a lot of hard work away from center stage. Tony considers impatience to be his weakness in the business world; but it would be hard to prove that point based on his odyssey to become an undefeated starter at Penn State.

"When Tony told me he wanted to play football at Penn State," Charles says, "I didn't really question it. Even at a young age, Tony would take his time and think things through. Mauresé and I knew that we would do whatever we could to make that possible."

After the couple enrolled Tony at the exclusive Phillips Academy prep school, Charles began a lobbying campaign on behalf of his eldest. He called to let Paterno know Tony was transferring from McDowell to Andover and he would be staying an extra year to better prepare his body for college football— hopefully at Penn State.

"I didn't want Tony to come to Penn State," Paterno recalls. "He already had a lot going for him. Harvard and Yale were very interested in him because of his scholastic achievement. At Andover, he was voted the outstanding student athlete; [U.S. President] George [H.W.] Bush, who is a good friend of mine, spoke well of him.

"And Charlie's calling me and telling me he wants to play for Penn State. I said, 'Charlie, he's not very big, I'm not sure he can play here. I'm not going to give him a chance.'"

Paterno's program was 20 years and a galaxy away from what it had been in the elder Pittman's era. Then, Paterno was building a nationally respected program. In 1990, the year Tony graduated from high school, Penn State had already won two national championships and was a mecca for some of the nation's most talented athletes.

It took some thought and a thorough review of Tony's high school performances, but Paterno decided to recruit him. Tony made the choice easy by finishing first in his class in academics and winning the Yale Bowl—an honor awarded to the member of the senior class who attained the highest proficiency in scholarship and athletics.

As if channeling the spirit of his aunt Rosalind, Tony's academic abilities were prodigious and stoked by an unyielding curiosity.

"The first thing that struck me about Tony was his academic preparation in coming to Penn State," remembers Lee Rubin. "I hosted Tony on his recruiting trip. I showed him around the campus. They put me with him because of my academic background. My father was a high school teacher. My brother went to Lehigh and Northwestern. He really had a desire to know more about the academics.

"It was very clear that Tony had a home life that strongly prepared him for success. Paterno is a master at recruiting the people that fit, and Tony fit the Penn State profile—they're not a turnaround organization. Tony was good at being himself; he tried to distance himself from the Pittman name, so to speak. He was adamant about making it on his own."

Tony's dream of playing for Penn State meant pursuing a course of action most high schoolers would consider nightmarish. He voluntarily chose an extra year of high school. A teenager, the age when a 30-minute wait for dinner is cause for rebellion and the full measure of 365 days in a year seems epoch, Tony waited a year for his chance. He waited a year to grow bigger; he waited a year to gain more experience; he waited a year because his father told him he wasn't ready for football at the Penn State level. The odds were enormous. Football is the most popular high school sport in the nation and Tony was one of 1.5 million youths playing junior high and high school football. Only 75,000 of them make it to the college level. Just a handful of those make it elite programs such as Penn State.

"We are allowed a total of 85 football scholarships," explains Penn State athletic director Tim Curley. "We have recruiting classes of 18 to 25 students coming in each year. These are the cream of the crop; they are the very high end of the whole recruiting process, and they have to meet academically stringent requirements for admission and attendance."

At the end of that long, long extra year, if Tony hadn't worked hard enough, there would be no Penn State. But his dream didn't wither.

"I gave him a scholarship," Paterno said.

Paterno redshirted Tony during his freshman year. A redshirt designation in college football means the coach has decided the athlete may attend classes, practices, and can even don a uniform, but will not participate in the sports season. By redshirting an athlete, the coach allows him to do a number of things—acclimate academically, acclimate athletically, or heal from an injury.

At one point, it became too much for Tony. Despite being a star offensive player in high school, Paterno, as is his wont, changed his position and made him a defender. It was one of the most physically challenging eras of his life. Every weekday during the football season, he sacrificed his body to bigger, stronger players. Picked himself off the turf bloodied and bruised and got back in line for more—with no hope of getting any playing time in his first year.

Like his father before him, he made a call home.

"Dad, I don't know why I'm not playing," he said. "I'm just as good as the guys ahead of me."

"Tony," Charles answered. "You can't be just as good as those players and expect Joe to make them sit. I wouldn't even do that for you. You've got to show him that you're better. Now, you get off the phone and call me back when you can tell me that you're better and not playing; then we've got something to talk about."

To earn the privilege of playing at Penn State, Tony was required to do something for which the past year had prepared him well—wait.

Down to Business	Penn State owes a debt of gratitude to Joe Paterno's father—and to Joe's misinterpretation of his father's advice.

"I was never gifted," Paterno says. "My dad used to tell me not to worry about it, just plug away. I'm not sure I took it in the way he meant it. I always thought 'plug away' meant to take care of the details. I worried about making sure everybody got to the field on time, making sure everyone knew the plays. Then winning football games would take care of itself."

Preparation Helps Overcome the Odds

The central theme of Penn State football—as coached by Joe Paterno—is that preparation can overcome odds. And odds are always something to consider. Any player who steps onto the playing field of a Big Ten football stadium on Saturday faces odds that he can't overcome alone. The muscle on showcase could probably lay a foundation for the Great Pyramid in an afternoon.

It's clear, on the face of it, that individual speed cannot overcome an entire team's collective swiftness; nor can one person's muscle trump the physical strength of an entire opposing team. A football coach's goal is to mold individual parts into a cohesive whole to improve his odds of winning. So should it be for a businessperson.

Raking Leaves and Learning Languages

It takes significant planning and psychological savvy to sand off the rough edges of individualism to create a successful football team. It requires an understanding of odds-making. It is a long, involved process. The same holds true for business.

Here are two quick analogies to consider when thinking of overcoming odds: raking leaves and learning a foreign language.

Remember those moments—perhaps chilled by fall winds—that you began an afternoon of raking fallen leaves? If you're like most people, at some point it seemed too great a task. Just having to bend down and drop the leaves into empty trash bags seemed to take hours. The dozens of empty plastic bags seem to mock you as you fill that first bag.

Or consider the dread of seeing that initial list of vocabulary words in the process of learning a foreign language. The references to present, past, and future tenses may seem too much for one mind to hold—after all, there's already a full set of language skills in there, right?

Raking leaves, learning a language, putting together a football team, and achieving a business goal all have in common the perception of being "too much" in the early stages. Too many leaves, too many words, too many rules—*It's too big a job.*

There is a monumental feel to the early stages of both the mundane task of raking leaves and the life-altering task of learning a new language. Whether you are drilling new words into a head that is already stuffed with English or spending a long afternoon doing yardwork, it's best to have a plan and manage your time well. Why? Because it is human nature to feel overwhelmed by anything that requires time and planning.

Plan with Passion

Planning can be a dry process—planning a budget for a distribution project, for instance. But it can also be part of a well-considered strategy, a passion for doing something. Never lose sight of that passion, no matter how pedestrian the planning may become. Tony Pittman's plan involved getting to Penn State by diligently working out and, where he had to, biding his time. Though he waited, he didn't stand still. He lifted weights in lonely weight rooms, ran miles and miles until his legs cramped, studied playbooks until his eyes blurred, and carefully assessed the competition.

When Charles was hired at Marine Bank in Erie, Pennsylvania, his plan was to engage the community, particularly the African American community.

Fred Rush, an Erie native who had walked on to the Lions football team when Pittman played, met Charles through Marine Bank.

"Charles came to Erie and he was such a gregarious guy," Rush recalls. "He was one of our best imports. He was always trying to do things; he was a planner, a real initiator. In the African American community in Erie, we have to be able to trust each other before we do anything else and trust comes from socialization. When Charles came to Erie, he worked at building a socialization network. We'd have meetings at the bank in the evening. Some of us who'd lived there for years finally got to know each other. He would organize field trips to Cleveland to see Marvin Gaye and Millie Jackson. He'd just jump in an RV and say, 'Let's go!'"

Erie County in the late 1970s and early 1980s had a population of about 280,000 people. Roughly 12,000 were African American—a 4.3 percent representation. Almost all of the area's African Americans lived in Erie, nicknamed the Flagship City. Erie had a population of roughly 100,000 people—the fourth most populous in Pennsylvania. By the time Charles took a position with Marine Bank, the city on the lake was losing jobs, industry, and young people, like much of the Rust Belt. Pop singer Billy Joel was singing about Allentown in his famous song lamenting central Pennsylvania's decline, but it easily could have been Erie. Erie had given the world Ann B. Davis, who played Alice on *The Brady Bunch*, America's first Homeland Security director Tom Ridge, and Eddie Klep, the first white man to play in baseball's Negro Leagues. Perhaps not knowing what to do with the gift, the world didn't have much to give back to Erie.

Still, if it was the picture of an urban area in decline, it never mattered to Charles. Erie became home and home was where he intended to place his heart.

"He was the first black man in banking I'd ever seen," Rush said. "There's a saying [in Erie] that Pennsylvania is Pittsburgh in the west, Philadelphia in the east—and Alabama in the middle. Most of the black executives I'd met would look for work in the two largest cities and the state capital and leave that middle alone. There was a lot of pressure on him, but he took everything well and he didn't take himself too seriously. He made an impact on Erie that is still here; it's a better community because he was here."

Bad Things Happen to Good People—Be Prepared

Charles's good fortune to be hired at Marine Bank came on the heels of what he saw as a negative event—the end of his pro football career. Paterno knew he had a young family to support and the money he made teaching (pro football was not as lucrative back in the early 1970s as it is today) was barely enough for his growing family. Paterno called in a favor. Edward "Ted" Junker III, a former football player and chair of the university's board of trustees, was the president of Marine Bank in Erie. Paterno asked if he would find a job for Charles. Junker agreed, and Charles left teaching for Marine Bank in 1973.

"I was a banker," he says. "I spent a lot of time studying; I researched credit card operations, which were just coming into play, and I studied state and federal regulations. I was transferring my skills from my sports career to my work career. I had every expectation of succeeding. I had won 29 straight games in high school, 30 in college, and I felt I had the discipline to learn what I needed to learn in this new field."

In 1975, after success with the bank's credit card operations, Pittman was promoted to an officer-level position. He was the only African American in the city of Erie with the power to lend a bank's money. In 1980, an African American–owned business caught his eye; it was a start-up and the first of its kind in northwest Pennsylvania. Its owners approached Marine Bank for a loan.

"A black banker lending to a black business," Pittman recalls. "I became very invested in its success. It got to the point that I was going past the guidelines with the amounts of money we loaned to it. But I hid it to try to give it more time to be successful. Unfortunately, I took a vacation, and when I came back from vacation, the company had been delinquent.

"Ted Junker was the president of the bank, the man who brought me in and had acted as my champion within the company. He called me on the carpet. I felt like I had let him down; I had disappointed him. He suggested I resign, which I did.

"I hadn't done anything wrong or illegal by going beyond the guidelines; but in the banking industry when a client doesn't pay, they take that personally."

Rush remembers that period and says the African American community was ready to take up arms over the dismissal.

"But Charlie didn't want us to make a big deal out of it," he says. "There was no outcry because he didn't want there to be one."

Don't Allow Adversity to Cause You to Second-Guess Yourself

Different personalities push themselves through tasks in different ways. Some make promises to themselves, some make threats. But whatever the personality, planning helps to achieve concrete goals. Paterno understands that aspect of human nature and has created a program that puts young people face to face with gargantuan tasks that force them to believe in themselves as part of a collective. Playing for Paterno is not about padding your individual statistics. Winning as part of a united team is what matters. Paterno grooms his teams to focus on the team's objective—winning. Individual achievement takes a backseat.

For example, Charlie Pittman's indoctrination into college life has much in common with the millions of freshmen who grow homesick and want to go home. Paterno salvaged his confidence with a well-timed pat on the back or supportive comment when he needed it most. As an adult, Pittman handled his own adversity head on. At Marine Bank he told the truth—he was fired. He then moved on.

Tony's decision to spend more time in high school and college could have changed on any of the 104 weekends that comprised those extra two years. He could have simply said, "This is too much," and walked away with a fine education, an unbruised body, an earlier entrance into the business world, and fond memories of high school football.

But Shakespeare had something to say about such fickleness in *Hamlet*, and it's likely Paterno would agree.

> Thus conscience does make cowards of us all;
> And thus the native hue of resolution
> Is sicklied o'er with the pale cast of thought,
> And enterprises of great pith and moment
> With this regard their currents turn awry,
> And lose the name of action.

Adversity diminishes the resolve of even the most fervent believers. Call it by its street name—fear. Fear is what separates undefeated teams from the rest of the pack—fear of failure, fear of having wasted time, fear of being fired. If you or your business never encounters adversity, then you and your business are rare beyond measure and deserve a refund of the price of this book. But for the 99.9 percent of the world that experiences downturns, ill winds, and misfortunes, embrace your adversity. You will never overcome it from a distance.

WINNING IN LIFE

"I don't think you have to annihilate or dominate in order to achieve victory. I'm the type that believes it's fine to win 15–14; you don't want to win 48–0. If you dominate, there is some teaching that's missing. In business, you don't want to annihilate either. When you're making money by doing all the wrong things—cheating, skirting the rules, abusing the labor force, shortchanging the product, you don't make it for long. I think of Penn State as an example. I want to be part of a business that's going to endure, constantly improve the product, and give back to the community. Leave the dirty tricks to others and you'll gain respect throughout your industry."

—Charles Pittman

CHAPTER 3

Goal Setting the Penn State Way

On December 30, 1967, the defense had set the tone for three quarters in a Gator Bowl that was all Penn State. The vaunted Florida State offense that featured flanker Ron Sellers was sputtering. Sellers had gained more yards via pass receptions than anyone in the nation that season. Florida State quarterback Kim Hammond was ranked number two in the country for total offense in 1967. But there was no offensive heat in the Florida night for the Seminoles. Head coach Bill Peterson was stalking the sideline and growling at anyone who came near. He had rejected a Liberty Bowl bid to accept this game, and his team was being demolished 17–0 with three quarters of play gone by. As the third quarter wound down, Penn State faced a fourth and one on its own 15-yard line. Though members of the punting squad looked like they would head onto the field, quarterback Tom Sherman and the rest of the offense stayed on the field. The players had talked Paterno into letting them go for the first down. One could almost hear a gasp from the Lions faithful. Failing to gain that yard would leave the Seminoles in the red zone. The gamble failed, and a reinvigorated Florida State went on to score a touchdown. Charlie fumbled the ensuing kickoff and the Seminoles scored another touchdown—14 points in 69 seconds. As time expired in the game, Florida State kicked a field goal to tie the score at 17–17.

In the heart of the turbulent 1960s, new Penn State head coach Joe Paterno found his trademark. In an era of pastels and psychedelia, Paterno decided to stand out in the most notable way possible—by being plain. Though he could have lobbied for names on the backs of jerseys, racing stripes, or golden helmets, Paterno chose to keep the plain-vanilla uniforms of Penn State's past as a statement. He had a goal. His goal was to push individualism toward a common goal. The plain uniforms were a part of that larger goal.

"Now, anyone who's played for Joe wouldn't think of getting rid of those plain uniforms," Charles says. "When we wore them, we were able to catch teams by surprise. They'd see our plain blue and white uniforms and our black shoes and think, 'These guys aren't so good; they're not so fast.' They underestimated us just because of the uniforms we wore.

"Penn State is unique in that regard. Paterno made us feel special and created a bond. In a sense, it was us against the world; that helped bond us together. But it's hard to understand that when you're a young man. In my sophomore year, for instance, I started growing a moustache—or trying to. Joe saw that and told me to shave it off. He said, 'You didn't have it when you came, so get rid of it.'"

Paterno had spent 16 seasons as an assistant to his friend and mentor, Rip Engle. In 1966, he became the Nittany Lions' head coach and the show was his alone. His first season would be a mediocre 5–5 affair, but the bespectacled Paterno saw only opportunity. By 1968, Paterno's first recruiting class was holding its own on the field.

Like Charlie Pittman, a coveted recruit who was his first choice for stocking his offensive backfield, Paterno was sensing the possibilities of his position. He could create any offensive and defensive schemes he desired, set any training schedules for his players, recruit however he chose, and fashion any legacy for the program.

Paterno, an Ivy League–educated Brooklynite of Italian descent, opted for a reality that didn't truly exist at big public schools like Penn State. He would set the Penn State program apart from other programs by embarking on his "Grand Experiment."

A hypercompetitive man, Paterno wanted to prove to the world that athletic success could be achieved by intelligent athletes who were true students. Paterno told the world, through the pages of *Sports Illustrated* and other major media, that his recruiting would target high-quality student-athletes, with the emphasis on student. Thus, the Grand Experiment was born.

And many scoffed. College football in the 1960s was dominated by programs that never saw a graduation rate they couldn't tunnel under. The concept of the boneheaded jock had taken hold, and visions of husky young men enrolling in basket-weaving classes danced in the minds of opportunistic football coaches.

By 1966 football had begun a rocket ride to popularity. Baseball was still king in the United States, but college football had 100 years of tradition and its intricately brutal dance of conquest and advancement was proving to be an easy sale to fans flush with cash in a plush economy.

Geography also played a part. The fastest, strongest athletes were recruited with a wink and a nod by grand programs in the South, Midwest, and Southwest. Eastern programs such as Penn, Harvard, and Brown were among the first to play the game, but had long since lost ground to schools such as Alabama, UCLA, Texas, Notre Dame, Oklahoma, USC, and others. A sort of consolation prize—the Lambert Trophy—was given annually to the best football team in the East.

Paterno inherited a well-tended program from Coach Engle that was mired in the past football glories of the fading East. For the new coach to spread talk about some Grand Experiment was considered foolhardy by many—even as they publicly lauded his commitment to scholarship. Paterno's principled stand could have been the sunset for Eastern football, but someone forgot to tell Joe.

"Whatever you do, you do trying to create a tradition," Paterno said. "We talk to people about the fact that we're conservative and we like team people. We're not looking for flashy people. I think people, every once in a while, need symbols to reinforce those sentiments."

Charlie's and Paterno's fates were on a collision course, and their collaboration would lay the foundation for a program that would become one of a handful of perennial elites in college football.

Winning football, Penn State style, means having nested goals—goals within goals—and achieving them in turn. Putting Paterno's goal of having a winning program into a rough equation looks something like this: recruit intelligent athletes willing to commit to his rules + prize collective effort over individual achievement + teach athletes the system + play strong schedule = winning program.

It's worth noting that the equation aims for winning football, not national championships. Famed college basketball coach John Wooden of UCLA was Paterno's opposite in that regard. Wooden used to write down his expectations for a particular season on a piece of paper, seal it an envelope, and share it with his team at the end of the year. On it, he might write "conference championship" or he might write "national championship." Unlike Paterno, he cast his gaze on the end result of a season and worked backwards.

That would be anathema to Paterno's methods. While Wooden's style was that of the grand architect envisioning the completed structure and then attending to the details, Paterno's style is more analogous to a bricklayer—lay the foundation correctly and the structure will be glorious. In his world, a winning program generates national championships.

And a by-product of recruiting those intelligent athletes is that those athletes become alumni who generally are successful and maintain support of the program. Each generation of players becomes a legion of well-spoken advocates, pillars of the community who praise the system.

"The program has been built on the family concept," says Penn State athletic director Tim Curley. "Coach Paterno stressed that from day one. We are family and want to treat each other that way.

As far as any legacy or success we have? Each year the incoming group has to have the responsibility and accountability to not let the sweat and tears of previous groups go in vain. That's why we have football spaces that are dedicated to former players. It's why we have such an active Letterman's Club; it's why our student-athletes and their families help the recruiting process by recommending our program."

One of the rituals for those former players is to return for April's Blue and White Game in Happy Valley. It is an intra-squad game that provides the first showcase for the newest iteration of the Nittany Lions. The game is a homecoming for both players and fans. Former players are put up in a stadium suite, fed well, and placed in the company of players from various eras.

In the stadium, fans are able to mingle with, and request autographs from, players from more than 40 years of Nittany Lions' football teams. Though he is now a successful media executive who is four decades removed from his college gridiron feats, fans still recognize Charles Pittman. Walking through the stadium to get to the elevator that leads to the former players' suite, fans still call his name and chase after him with blue markers, helmets and jerseys in tow to be signed.

He always obliges, even when signing one means signing 10. The younger fans who notice the tall, trim man signing autographs typically ask the question: "Who is he?"

"He's Charlie Pittman. He was a running back for Paterno's first teams."

Invariably, another helmet or jersey is shoved into his face. And another. He's found that the art of being a celebrity—even in these very specific circumstances—lies in making the experience positive for all concerned. Pittman has perfected a breakaway from autograph seekers reminiscent of his dashes on the field—smooth and quick.

"One more," he says to no one in particular. He accepts the proffered item, the "one more" he promised, signs it, takes another, signs it, and begins a quick walk away, a smile on his face. *Always underpromise and overdeliver* is one of his favorite sayings.

"Thank you!" he says over his shoulder.

As the 1967 season neared its end, Paterno knew he had something rare—a young, poised team. His defensive backfield was drum-tight and all the kids seemed to be taking to his program well.

Such cohesion seemed to be a minor miracle at a time when America had apparently decided to tear itself apart at the seams. These kids—baby boomers, the magazines called them—were inundated by Vietnam, the civil rights movement, women's lib, the SDS, the SLA, a burgeoning push for free drugs and sex, and a consumer marketing campaign unseen in the likes of human history. Everyone wanted a piece of them and their time: the draft board, Dr. Martin Luther King Jr., Gloria Steinem, Abbie Hoffman, and Madison Avenue.

The African American kids especially were trapped between a rock and a hard place. Central Pennsylvania had a small African American population, and the school's student body was less than 1 percent black in the mid-1960s. They were being asked to enjoy the college experience and represent Penn State well when there were ugly pockets of racism that limited the scope of their college years.

Penn State recruited African American athletes relatively early in its history, but those earlier athletes dealt with an even more unvarnished racism since they had no fully-formed civil rights movement to support them. Lenny Moore, who sang the siren's song for Charlie, along with Roosevelt Grier, Jesse Arnelle, and Charlie Janerette, encountered enormous difficulties as African American athletes at Penn State in the 1950s. They had few places where they could go for something as simple as a haircut; many campus hangouts were off-limits to them.

Lou Prato, author of *The Penn State Football Encyclopedia*, said African American football players had 25 years of history at the school by the time the class of 1966 arrived on campus.

"Our very first black athlete at Penn State was [football player] Dave Alston, who came aboard in 1941," Prato says. "He died of a tonsillectomy operation in 1942. He had a great academic background and came from a steel mill town in western Pennsylvania. Then there was Wally Triplett, who came to town fresh out of high school in Philadelphia. Wally had to go through a lot of hell to be the first starter on the Nittany Lions football team."

Those pioneer players often had to find justice on the football field when they couldn't find it in the nation at large.

"In 1946, the team cancelled a game against Miami because Miami wouldn't allow Negro players [Triplett and Dennie Hoggard] on its field," Prato says. "It's ironic because Miami recruited [Triplett], they just didn't know he was black. There was a lineman on the 1946 team, a fellow by the name of Red Moore, that Wally remembers sticking up for him. Red said he played against Negro players in high school and didn't think they should segregate the game."

Hoggard and Triplett, who would go on to be drafted by the NFL in 1949, became the first African Americans to play in the Cotton Bowl on January 1, 1948.

By 1967, race was just one of many explosive issues facing the nation. As America's controversies swirled around them, Paterno's squad seemed to possess a single-minded focus: winning games. Their six victories meant the team's final two regular-season contests would decide whether the season would end in a bowl game and validation of Paterno's trust or in a hard reminder that these were young, unseasoned players.

The team faced Ohio University on November 18 and Charlie was growing comfortable with his new one-handed carrying style; he had five games under his belt without a fumble. Though he rushed for about a hundred yards against Ohio, the story of that game proved to be the play of his defensive teammates. Jim Kates, his roommate and a defensive starter, would be bragging about his defensive mates later that evening. He would have much to brag about since the Lions' defense alone would outscore the Bobcats.

Sophomore defensive back Bob Capretto started the run by intercepting an Ohio pass and running it in for a 50-yard touchdown. Linebacker Dennis Onkotz returned a punt 56 yards for a touchdown and defensive end Frank Spaziani blocked a punt and scored a 26-yard touchdown. Defensive players scored 21 points on the three plays. The final score of 35–14 was the team's sixth straight win with just one game left.

That game might as well have been labeled as an exclamation point. It was an emphatic win over the University of Pittsburgh that saw Penn State's junior quarterback Tom Sherman in great form. He threw four touchdowns against a beleaguered Panthers secondary.

If this group of Super Sophomores had been waiting to exhale, then this game provided a cathartic exhalation that carried them to a bowl game and a Lambert Trophy. They were for real, and even Coach Paterno had to smile at how well these pups handled the pressure of their first season. Against Pittsburgh, bruising sophomore fullback Don Abbey scored twice and kicked six PATs for one of his best games of the season.

As the clock wound down on the 42–6 victory, Charlie walked over to Abbey and slapped him hard on the shoulder pads.

"Great game, Don! Great game!"

Both knew there would be one more game—a bowl game—and that made their grins that much wider.

Tony Pittman's routine was one that stretched back to his freshman year in high school. He worked out with weights, ran, studied, and worked on his football IQ. Though his coursework was challenging, Tony had been well prepared for college work at

Andover. Here, football was the X factor. Even though he was a redshirt freshman he still had to keep in game shape—Paterno's eyes were everywhere. More important, he was living the dream he'd had since his father first began telling him about wearing No. 24, about the time the Nittany Lions scored against 12 big Kansas Jayhawks, about the significance of plain uniforms.

Most children were told bedtime stories; Tony remembers his stories were sandwiched between game plans. He knew his athletic destiny would fall within the blue lines of Beaver Stadium, and he had made it.

Phil Collins, a Cinnaminson, New Jersey, native who was one of 19 children, was a classmate of Tony's. Collins, a split end who was also redshirted his freshman year, became good friends with Tony. Collins's family was creating its own legacy at Penn State. His brothers Gerry and Andre also played for Paterno. Andre played outside linebacker for the Washington Redskins team that won the Super Bowl after the 1991 season. An amazing five of the seven Collins boys played for Penn State—Andre, Gerry, Phil, Jason, and Aaron.

Phil Collins was impressed with Tony's work ethic, which matched his own.

"The guy was always prepared," Collins said. "It didn't matter if he was starting a game or not, he was ready to go."

Paterno noticed that trait as well.

"Tony never came to the practice with the idea he wasn't a first stringer," Paterno recalls. "Tony was not shy. I've always admired him for that. He'd come into my office and say, 'Joe, I'm better than that guy.' I should have started him sooner, but I got a lot of negative feedback because of his size."

The Lions were a strong team in Tony's freshman year. Though they began the 1990 season with two close losses to Texas and USC, they went on a nine-game tear the rest of the way.

They lost to two out of the three ranked opponents they faced in 1990, but the lone win was a good one. On November 17, they pulled off an upset against number one-ranked Notre Dame. For Tony, it was sweeter—times 10—than a McDowell victory over Cathedral Prep. The only thing missing was being on the field.

Penn State's Nittany Lions faced their old bowl nemesis, seventh-ranked Florida State, in the Blockbuster Bowl on December 28. The Seminoles won by the score of 24–17, sending the Lions home with a 9-3 record and an Associated Press ranking of 11th in the nation.

Tony wasn't permitted to dress for that game and the loss hit him hard—he was a student of the team's history. Still, even with the loss he permitted himself a personal smile. Next year, 1991, he would cast off that proverbial redshirt and be in the thick of things. He vowed to spend a little extra time in the weight room the next day.

The coincidence is not lost on Charles and Tony that they both got their first starts as a result of injuries to other players. Campbell's injury in 1967 cleared the way for Charlie, and Shelly Hammonds, Penn State's starting cornerback, injured his hamstring in 1992, providing an opportunity for Tony. So, on October 24, 1992, Tony started his first game against the West Virginia Mountaineers, a team against which his father had had great success. Tony had a strong game as well. All the waiting and practice paid off handsomely when he intercepted a pass from quarterback Jake Kelchner—a Notre Dame transfer. The Lions won in a walk, 40–26. Hammonds returned for the next game and Tony was a backup again. But great things were on the horizon.

Down to Business   Joe Paterno doesn't spend any time second-guessing his decisions. Some might argue that doesn't include Florida State's famous comeback in the 1967 Gator Bowl. It's true that Paterno has frequently described that decision to go for it on a fourth and one on his own 15 as "boneheaded." But Charles Pittman contends the players talked him into it against his better judgment.

Not one time in the ensuing decades has Paterno ever corroborated that it was the players' decision, for a number of reasons—first among them is loyalty. It's a coaching axiom that victories belong to the players and losses belong to the coaches. Paterno may be tough and autocratic with his players but his loyalty is unwavering. Exposing his players to ridicule for a boneheaded play is out of bounds.

Do Your Homework

Preparation is a hallmark of Penn State football and college football in general. Opponents are studied rigorously and it's normal for players to spend as much time in the film room studying video as they do in the weight room. Sufficient preparation means you don't have to second-guess yourself.

Don't Confuse Adjustments with Second-Guessing

At halftime of each of the more than 500 games Paterno has coached, he and his staff have implemented adjustments and corrections to their game plans. A player might be having a career game and require more attention, or the execution of some set plays aren't getting the results anticipated. Those are corrections based on the information presented. Second-guessing is an acknowledgment that you did something wrong. It was the wrong play. It was the wrong game plan. These statements indicate something wrong with the preparation, not necessarily the plan.

Ron Bracken, sports editor for the *Centre Daily Times* newspaper, believes that Paterno's consistency borders on superstition.

"It's okay. You know what you're getting; but it's not okay because you know what you're getting," Bracken said. "He's a creature of habit. There are things he's said, stories he's told so many times, that I just number them. A lot of coaches and athletes are superstitious. But he has adapted. He's such a control freak; his strategy is to make sure you take care of kicking and don't beat yourself on defense. But he's adjusted—he's had to. Modern college football is a more wide open type of game. There's so much speed on offense now. You can't take your offense and be conservative, count on going 80 yards in 15 plays. With the athletes of today, they might go 80 yards on two plays."

The last word on second-guessing goes to Tony Pittman, by way of 19th-century poet-editor-essayist-diplomat James Russell Lowell: "Lowell wrote, and I agree, that 'the foolish and the dead alone never change their opinions.'"

Why Should I Avoid Second-Guessing?

In business, an example of second-guessing is telling yourself that you will never achieve that promotion. Second-guessing is counterproductive because its only goal is to plant doubt in your mind. The initial doubt is a bamboo shoot that is then watered daily with a stream of supporting doubt: *The boss hates me. I can't do this job. I'll probably get fired.*

The effect of such negative thinking on the football field and in business is devastating. So many turning points in business and sports come down to a single moment—a goal line stand, a big presentation. Negative thoughts are metaphorical tacklers dragging you down before you achieve your goal.

In the vernacular of sports, once that happens, doubt "owns you."

Tony Pittman is an example of the resolve it takes to achieve a goal. It is not a superhuman resolve—he was often frustrated not to be playing. His father recalls a time or two when he needed cheering up or commiseration. And there were days when a break from the grind would have felt heavenly. Like any human being, he toughed through the hard times that he could and sought help when the weight seemed too great. He'd call his mother and father; he'd talk to Paterno and mention how well he'd done in practice. He'd read books.

When in Doubt, Read Something Inspiring

"The book that affected me in college was *Candide* by Voltaire. I thought that was so interesting; he really attacked the issue that people want all of the things in their lives in neatly packaged outcomes. The message I got from *Candide* was that this is the best of all possible worlds, it must be part of a master plan; I can't worry about the patterns of the world, I've got to tend to my own garden.

"For some reason, even though it was all those years ago, that one has stuck with me. Anyone's star rises; you feel some days everything is great. Other days you want to jump off a cliff. Still, no matter what you do, whether it feels right or feels wrong, you've got to somehow maintain the top priorities you've decided on. Other things will eventually take care of themselves."

Another nugget from Voltaire: "Chance is a word devoid of sense; nothing can exist without a cause."

Be an Amazing Person

Americans have a love-hate relationship with egotistical people. Donald Trump, Deion Sanders, and Muhammad "I am the greatest" Ali all have contingents of people who despise them and those who adore them. It is the nature of fame, particularly sports and entertainment fame, that it requires some ego to handle the pressure.

As the head of 20 newspapers, four shoppers, and three phone directories, Charles Pittman has thousands of people who know his name and are affected by his decisions. It is a valid strategy to be a feared leader—Machiavelli recommends it—but Charles has chosen to be what he calls a "servant leader."

Mary Junck, CEO of Lee Enterprises and Charles's former boss, said she greatly appreciated his leadership style when he was at Lee.

"Charlie Pittman makes your heart sing," she said when describing his management style. "His objective is to inspire those who work for him to do the best they can by helping them be the best they can be."

That relationship requires Pittman to carefully consider his actions, which means second-guessing can be doubly harmful. Subordinates have effusive praise for his style of leadership.

John Humenik, former editor of the *Quad-City Times* in Davenport, Iowa, recalls working for Charles.

"A day doesn't go by that I don't think warmly about Charles Pittman," Humenik said. "How fortunate I was to be his editor at the *Quad-City Times*. How fortunate I am to be counted among his friends...his passion for life is infectious. It's rare that a speech by Charles doesn't contain an empowering message about 'getting better every day.'"

Belong to an Organization You Believe In

Ron Bracken suggests that fitting the right people in the right place is a cornerstone of Penn State's success.

"The quality of the athletes as people is one thing that sets the program apart," Bracken says. "The vast, vast majority of the athletes that come here are good people. I couldn't name 10 people over all these years that I didn't like. I've done countless number of sit-down interviews with them and I generally get a pretty good feel for them. The huge majority, you come away impressed with them."

Bracken says the father-son nature of the Pittmans' story may be repeated at other schools, but it has a unique twist at Penn State.

"I think that every school has situations like that," he said. "Legacies are what they call them. Every fall those kinds of stories surface. Programs across the nation expect the son to go there if the dad went there. The Suheys are another great story; they go back to 1919 with the school. What makes Penn State unique is that fathers and sons might play for the same coach. I can't think of any other school where that might be the case. The other schools have loyalty to the program, not the coach."

It's All about Confidence

Confidence in business is won no more easily than it is on the football field, and it will be assaulted just as much by bigger, stronger, faster, richer, or smarter competitors.

Your confidence, like Charlie's and Tony's confidence, should be based on something that you have worked on. As a running back, it was obvious that running would be a means to an end for success. Adapt that strategy to your business situation—if you are a salesperson, you might cultivate contacts or a comfort with creating relationships with strangers. If you are an engineer, reviewing project specs might be your way of building confidence.

World-class motivational speaker Walter Bond, a former NBA player, has this suggestion for those in sales: "Do not consider yourself well-read in sales, or marketing, or management, until you have read 2,500 books on sales. Not magazines, not articles—books," he says. Bond sets a high threshold, but he stands by it because he's had to read that many books on motivational speaking.

"If you don't," he says with a grin, "you suck."

The common theme is to get better each day and, most important, to recognize your seven-yards-per-carry days. Seven-yards-per-carry days are the days when you minimize the positive things you do. That's a mistake you should never make.

Who's Your Idol?

One of the smartest things Charlie did to overcome his lack of knowledge about high-level football was to make an idol of Lenny Moore, already a proven success. In business, you can call them mentors or champions, but the effect is the same. Idols, mentors, champions all show you how it's done. They provide a measuring stick to gauge progress and success.

You can do that. You don't have to choose a jersey number, just choose to be confident.

> WINNING IN LIFE
> "A business wins with its people. So I believe it's very important that you tell people the truth about how good they are and you challenge them. That helps their confidence and turns potential into reality. I think sometimes a great potential is one's biggest enemy. Unless you deliver it, it wears heavily on you."
> —Charles Pittman

PART II

The Blue Line

CHAPTER 4

Your Only Two Choices Are to Get Better or Get Worse

Miami on January 1, 1969, the Nittany Lions were trailing Kansas 14–7 in the Orange Bowl at the end of the 1968 season. The Jayhawks, led by quarterback Bobby Douglass and crafty running backs John Riggins and Donnie Shanklin, were tricky to contain, but the Penn State defense was rock solid. With 1:16 left in the fourth quarter, Lions defensive back Neal Smith came out of a 10-man rush to block a Jayhawks punt on the Penn State 49-yard line. On the first offensive play after that recovery, quarterback Chuck Burkhart hit receiver Bobby Campbell for a 48-yard pass play that took the ball to Kansas's 3-yard line. Three plays later, Burkhart surprised Coach Joe Paterno and running back Charlie Pittman by keeping the ball on a scissors slant over left tackle and running it in for a touchdown. No one was more surprised by the play than Burkhart, who had been a functional, play-not-to-lose quarterback, rather than a go-for it-all gambler. But Burkhart saw the KU linemen keying on Charlie and knew the play Paterno called wouldn't work but didn't have time to call an audible. "I thought we had fumbled," Charlie said. "Then I was tackled and then I saw Chuck score." The three plays leading up to the score had been hectic and intense. Linemen and blockers were screaming at each other: "Have you got your man?" "I got my man!" "Do you have your man?" The Jayhawks seemed to be everywhere at once. With Burkhart's touchdown, Penn State needed a two-point conversion to take the game. But a pass from Burkhart to Campbell was batted down, causing hundreds of Kansas fans to storm the

67

field. The Nittany Lions' winning streak was snapped at 18 and several hundred miles away, Eric Pittman, Charlie's 11-year-old brother, was crying in front of the family's TV set in Baltimore. But a red flag thrown by an official called the play back. Kansas had had 12 men on the field for the entire series of downs that originated on the three-yard line—including Burkhart's touchdown. KU linebacker Rick Abernathy never left the field when his replacement came in. After the penalty, Campbell ran around the left end behind three solid blocks to give the Nittany Lions the win.

The ascension of Nittany Lions football didn't come without turmoil. In fact, the program's first undefeated season came during a year when key players were being pulled in different directions by social forces. Charlie was at the center of one of those conflicts, and his decision could have substantially changed the arc of the program's history. He faced the same pressures as Olympic 200-meter sprinters Tommie Smith and John Carlos—who were banned from the 1968 Olympics and stripped of their medals for making Black Power salutes on the medal stand.

It was a year of choices, and for 20-year-old Charlie they were the hardest choices imaginable. How does one choose between a team and a race; between a principled protest and a sport that has provided a college education?

Charlie's choice was set in motion on April 4, 1968, when Reverend Martin Luther King Jr. was shot to death in Memphis, Tennessee. Riots broke out in 125 cities across the country when the news reached African American neighborhoods.

Charlie's hometown of Baltimore was one of the last cities to experience riots, but when it flashed on April 6—it flashed hot.

On a warm Saturday, thousands of people took to the streets, some crying, some yelling, all angry. As soon as he was notified, Maryland governor Spiro Agnew called in thousands of National Guard troops and 500 Maryland state police officers to confront the rioters. But the force of the mob's anger washed over the troops and grew stronger. Seeing what looked like a military presence in their neighborhoods, even more people joined in.

Maddened by King's murder and distrustful of this governmental show of power, rioters tried to tear the city down with bricks, torches, iron bars, or anything they could lay their hands on. Over the course of the riot, more than a thousand fires would be set. Within 24 hours, Agnew called U.S. president Lyndon B. Johnson for support for his overmatched forces. Johnson ordered the 18th Airborne from Fort Bragg, North Carolina, to Baltimore. Five-thousand soldiers—paratroopers, combat engineers, artillerymen, and snipers—descended on the city. A light infantry brigade was added two days later as the riots continued to grow.

Soldiers used bayonets to subdue the rioters and military aircraft circled Baltimore, dropping what were called "chemical dispersers" on the city. Between the smoke from the fires of burning buildings and the swirling clouds of tear gas, the streets of Baltimore could have passed for war-torn Vietnam.

By the following Saturday, an uneasy peace took hold. As the violence waned, police and military made the bulk of their arrests—more than 3,000 people. The detainees were tagged with bracelets and transported to jail cells in cattle trucks. By the time it was over, six people were dead, 700 were injured, 4,500 were arrested, and $13.5 million in property was destroyed. Agnew, who had been seen as a racial moderate in the state, wasted no time in assessing blame for the riots.

He blamed the city's African American leaders, saying, "I call on you to publicly repudiate all black racists. This, so far, you have been unwilling to do." King's body had not yet been buried.

Two months later, on June 6, 1968, presidential candidate Robert F. Kennedy would also be cut down by a bullet.

This was the poisonous climate that gripped the nation when Charlie and 100 other Penn State players returned to campus for spring football.

Paterno had spent the off-season at dozens of events explaining the "boneheaded" play in the third quarter of the Gator Bowl that led to a 17–17 tie with Florida State. Maybe the effort of those explanations wore on him; maybe it was the sour mood of a nation in the midst of a cultural war. Whatever the reason, his practices became even tougher for the players, and he was rarely satisfied with their efforts—particularly those of the offensive squad.

"We can't run two plays in a row [in practice] without busting one," Paterno moaned to the media. As the season opener against Navy loomed, Paterno's mood darkened. Football seemed to be the last thing on the minds of several of his players and that wouldn't cut it.

Paterno had a rule: a blue painted border surrounded the football field that the team practiced on. The rule was not to cross the blue line unless you were 100 percent ready. If you were injured or in any way distracted, you stayed off the football field. So, Paterno could not accept anything less than 100 percent focus. Certainly, the 1960s were difficult times, but so were Nittany Lions practices. Paterno wasn't being insensitive to the times; he is a highly educated man who has always professed an unabashed love for the American Experiment, so the assassinations and riots shook him deeply. Still, he was a football coach and a teacher. If he couldn't explain how such a thing could happen in America, at least he could show these kids that they had choices.

His kids would play football because that was the corner of the American Dream they signed up for; and if they were going to play, they might as well play well.

Charlie believed the same thing; spring football's pain and violence served as both a cross to bear and a salve for his aching soul. But it was difficult to get the images of a burning west Baltimore out of his head; and returning to a place named Happy Valley seemed surreal. The fact that some of the businesses in Happy Valley were still segregated stung even more.

But he couldn't forget that he was succeeding in the classroom, helped by the efforts of speech and English instructors who were white. He refused to demonize all white people—it didn't make sense. Most of his football brothers were white guys, good guys with whom he had accomplished great things.

And there was always Paterno to talk to; at the least Joe would never feed him BS.

Charlie's idol, Lenny Moore, had called Paterno a good man and that was all there was to say on the matter. Back in the 1950s when Moore was a star, race made his world even more claustrophobic than Charlie's.

"Rip, Joe, Earl Bruce, they were there for us," Moore told a sportswriter. "They were straight with us, fair and honest all the way down the line."

Charlie needed that fairness and honesty. Away from the streets of Baltimore and the husks of neighborhood stores that would never open again, he was starting to find peace. He might never understand the events of the past spring and summer, but he would learn from them. He wouldn't let the dream of either martyr die.

His gift was running the football and he would fly at every opportunity. He wanted America to see a young black man living his own dream on his own terms. Smart, athletic, and dedicated— Charlie and Penn State were a fit. It wasn't perfect by any means, but he believed in the integrity of the program.

And Paterno believed in him.

"I remember thinking when we were recruiting Charlie that this was a kid who had a lot to offer the community," Paterno recalls. "Black or white, athlete or nonathlete, Charlie Pittman is a winner. I know with a lot of African American athletes there is so much emphasis on making it in athletics that they don't take advantage of the other talents these kids might have, talents that might benefit the community at large. I wanted to make sure he understood he could have an impact."

A Season of Choices—1968

Navy

On September 21, the first day of fall, the Nittany Lions faced Navy. Paterno was a bundle of nerves at the opening kickoff. These Nittany Lions were a good team—he knew football too well not to know that—but they were still young and every day seemed to bring a new distraction. Paterno had lost steady quarterback Tom Sherman to graduation and was relying on a slight junior named Chuck Burkhart to take the snaps.

Navy had beaten the Lions in 1967; if they did it again, the season would be a crapshoot. History is littered with up-and-down college football teams who take down juggernauts and lose to cream puffs. Those kinds of teams age a coach beyond his years. Paterno had looked long and hard into the collective soul of this team and he still wasn't sure whether last year's 8–2–1 record had been the result of a young team with something to prove or if this group of players was something truly special.

By the time the Lions stood across the Beaver Stadium field from head coach Bill Elias's Navy team, they were wound tight. Paterno had ridden them hard in the preseason and the players were eager to take their energy out on an opponent instead of each other.

From the game's opening minutes, Charlie had his way with Navy's defenders. He would finish the game with 112 yards that barely winded him. More than half of that yardage came on a single run that he broke for 57 yards and a touchdown. Indoctrinated in the Paterno system, Charlie left half a dozen Middies defenders in the dust of his run. With the crowd screaming his name and going wild in the stands, he squelched his youthful impulse to celebrate: he calmly flipped the ball to the referee and trotted back to the huddle.

The Penn State defense busied itself by driving Navy's quarterback, Mike McNallen, to distraction. It was as if the off-season had simply been an extended halftime for the Rover Boys. They were ravenous and an ambulatory meal had stumbled into their lair. The Penn State defense intercepted five passes, recovered four Navy fumbles, and held the Midshipmen's offense to an anemic total of seven yards. The Lions' 31–6 margin of victory could have been greater if Paterno had not called off the dogs—a habit of his in blowout games, one that years later would arguably cost him a national championship.

Nine games, no losses, and a jump in the AP rankings from number 10 to number four—Penn State football had hit the big time. In fact, the success of the 1967 season had attracted the attention of two high school running backs who were now show-ing promise on the freshman team—Lydell Mitchell and Franco Harris, both from New Jersey. Paterno's Grand Experiment, which many assumed would take years to come to fruition—if it blos-somed at all—was blooming.

Between games, Charlie's biggest concern was keeping his weight up. He despised lifting weights because he felt being too muscular would slow him down. His running style was based on long strides that required elasticity—not massive muscles. Occasionally, a strength coach could coerce him into lifting some weights for his arms or chest, but never his legs. Because he ran constantly, his weight was stuck in the low 180s. His preference would have been to play at 190 to have a least a little more padding for the hits he took on the field. It would have helped if he had a greater appetite, but his inclination toward overeating ran neck and neck with his desire to lift weights.

"At the training table, they'd give me three steaks and I'd eat one and give two away," he recalls.

Kansas State

Thin as he was, he still managed to give defenses fits, and after the Navy game, the Kansas State coaches were preparing for him. On the plains of Manhattan, Kansas, Kansas State coaches were creating scout teams that featured faux Charlie Pittmans—young players who were asked to run the ball like Penn State's Pittman. It had been Charlie's old job—to give the defense an opportunity to figure out a way to stop a premier running back.

When the fourth-ranked Lions faced Kansas State at Penn State's Beaver Stadium on September 28, they were expected to win. Kansas State was a Big 8 team, but its program at that time was not among the elite in that proud football conference. They had a new 35,000-seat stadium, Bill Snyder Family Football Stadium, which would fit inside of Beaver Stadium. In this game, Paterno faced something new from his players and Nittany Lions fans—overconfidence.

"You still gotta play the game!" he shouted during the week's practice. "They're not going to roll over for you!"

The young coach was right to be concerned. The Wildcats jumped to a 9–7 lead before Penn State could spring a big play. Campbell busted a trap play for a 56-yard gain and was chased down at the Kansas State 28-yard line. The tackle separated his shoulder. Charlie finished the series by scampering in on a five-yard run. Once again, the defensive squad locked down the opposing team; Smear, Reid, Onkotz and a tough sophomore linebacker named Jack Ham did much of the damage. The Lions won 25–9, learned a lesson about being overconfident against an opponent, and stretched their unbeaten streak to 10 games over two seasons.

Bloody Tuesday after the Kansas State game was particularly gruesome. Paterno wanted to teach his team a lesson, it seemed. "Bad Rad" Radakovich, the linebackers' coach, was a free spirit who never wore socks; but on that Tuesday—a game week Tuesday—he was less free spirit and more specter of doom. He worked his charges into such a frenzy that when they were doing "Oklahoma Drills," one-on-one drills against running backs, the hits felt like game hits. Charlie had already learned to...*accentuate* his accounts of the severity of his injuries and was able to beg off some of the drills.

West Virginia

The October 5 game against the West Virginia Mountaineers proved to be an exercise in efficiency. Though the Mountaineers would score 20 points—the second highest total scored against the Lions' defense all season—the victory was never truly in jeopardy. Charlie's game was solid as the Lions won 31–20. His stats were beginning to look gaudy. By season's end, he would rush for a team-leading 950 yards and a 5.1 yards-per-carry average. He would also score 14 touchdowns and lead the team in scoring by a wide margin, 84 points to second place Campbell's 44 points.

It was the October 12 game against UCLA that was a red-letter day for the Lions. Though the Bruins had lost Beban, their Heisman-winning quarterback, they were still UCLA. Paterno needed no motivational magic to get his team ready to play. But there were other forces at work that were affecting his budding star.

"There was a lot of campus unrest and black students were taking over buildings to protest," Pittman recalls. "There weren't very many black students, so the protests were generally about how black students were treated on campus; how there were no black members of the faculty. They approached me to protest with them.

"They said that if I would lead them, it would make the administration listen. I was troubled by all of this. I really didn't know what to do, whether to join in, support my race, and put my football team at risk."

Like Lenny Moore a generation before, Pittman sought Paterno's counsel.

"Joe," Charlie said in Paterno's office. "They want me to take over a campus building. If I don't, I'm selling out my race, but if I do, then I'm putting the football team at risk."

"Charlie," Paterno said. "Make a decision to do more. They want to take over a building in some kind of symbolic protest. You can do more to help the situation by doing well on the football team. That will do more to solve the problems they're protesting than taking over a building for an afternoon or a couple of days."

Years later Paterno acknowledges the pressures on his first All-American running back.

"We only had five or six black kids on the team," Paterno recalls. "In the summertime, so much stuff was going on, but Charlie always spoke up [about racial issues]. He wasn't a yes man; when he thought I was saying or doing something that might cause problems, he'd say, 'Coach, you're treading on thin ice there.' Charlie was motivated to be a leader on the team."

Paterno's advice seemed logical to Charlie. He steeled his courage and told the protest group that he wouldn't be joining them. He focused his energy on preparing for UCLA.

UCLA

On game day, the Lions' defenders exploded against the Bruins from the opening kickoff, often stranding them deep in their own territory. Ham blocked a punt in the game's second period and Kates scooped it up, taking it in for a TD from the 36-yard line.

Charlie wouldn't be outdone by his roommate. He broke a couple of tackles to complete a wild 28-yard touchdown run. The Lions buried the Bruins, 21–6. Paterno was beginning to notice a pattern. Charlie seemed to be even more productive when he was under pressure.

That pressure didn't abate after the game; Charlie had to deal with more controversy.

"We beat UCLA and we were the number three team in the country, so there was a rally to celebrate," Pittman recalls. "The same group that approached me earlier wanted me to boycott the team and the rally. I told them I couldn't do that. I supported their aims, but I supported my team, too. Saying no to that group was a burden I carried the rest of the time I was there. But the school had begun to change me. I arrived at Penn State as a very shy, underexposed kid from inner-city Baltimore. I was receiving an education, I was on my way to becoming an All-American, I was learning there are a lot of hard choices to make in life."

While Charlie wrestled with those choices, Paterno wrestled with some choices of his own. He had decided on a quarterback (six of his starters had been quarterbacks in high school) and his decision set off a wave of criticism from fans: *Burkhart is too slow. His arm is no good.*

"They said he couldn't do anything well," Pittman recalls. "But Chuck knew how to win. He never beat himself."

Boston College

Tom Sherman's absence was especially felt when the Lions played at Boston College on October 26. Boston College wasn't considered a real threat to State, but Burkhart had a hard time getting his feet under him. He completed just one of 11 passes as the first half was ending. Penn State had a 3–0 lead and no momentum. Then, Kwalick, the tight end, got the Lions' blood going with a spectacular falling catch on the Eagles' 31-yard line. He followed that up with a touchdown. Cherry rushed for a touchdown and Kwalick caught the two-yard conversion pass. In a matter of minutes, Penn State was up 17–0. The defense earned its first shutout as Penn State won 29–0.

The season was rolling along like the 11:15 PRR to Harrisburg.

Their next game, a homecoming game, would be against Army. The Cadets would surely offer a stronger test; many considered them the second best team in the East—after Penn State. They were dangerous: loaded both offensively and defensively. They had struggled early in the season and they had something to prove. Penn State would be the highest ranked foe they would face all season. The same week the Lions played Boston College, the Cadets demolished Duke 57–25 behind the six touchdowns scored by halfback Lynn Moore and fullback Chuck Jarvis.

Army

Army did prove to be tough, and it didn't help that Paterno's instincts were just a hair off during the game. On one play in the first half, when the Lions held a 9–0 lead with a fourth and one on the Cadets' 19-yard line, Paterno waved off both a field goal and a run and ordered a long pass from Burkhart. The pass fell incomplete. A few possessions later, he called for a sweep instead of heading inside where Campbell had been having good luck all game.

With each failed attempt, the Cadets were emboldened. The score tightened to 16–7 as the fourth quarter began. But in the paraphrased words of the Bard, immortal New York Yankees' pitcher Lefty Gomez, "Sometimes it's better to be lucky than good."

When a Lions field-goal attempt fell short near the end zone, the ball hit an Army player's foot and Penn State recovered, leading to a touchdown.

With three minutes to play in the fourth quarter, Army was still within sight of a win, trailing just 22–17. The Cadets went for an onside kick that both teams pounced on, but it ended up in the hands of Kwalick, who took the ball 53 yards for the score, giving the Lions a 28–17 advantage. Army, game until the end, scored again with less than two minutes in the game. The final score of 28–24 meant Paterno's team was unbeaten in 14 games.

It was official. This team was something special.

With such a talented team, Paterno decided he would try some new offensive schemes against Miami (FL), their upcoming opponent. He shifted some of his offensive linemen to create an unbalanced line, an effort to entice Miami's defense.

Paterno was playing chess now, testing not just his opponent, but his own players. The intelligence he sought in his athletes lent itself well to adaptability on the football field.

Miami

They played the Hurricanes on November 9 at Beaver Stadium, and players and coaches both were excited to see how the game plan would play itself out. The excitement didn't last long.

Paterno scrapped the new scheme soon after the Hurricanes took a 7–0 lead on a 78-yard pass play. But he ordered the offensive team to continue to run its plays away from the Hurricanes' 6'7", 220-pound defensive end known as the "Mad Stork"—Ted Hendricks. Hendricks, who would go on to a productive 15-year pro career, was a black hole for offensive plays.

It wasn't until Miami's other defensive end, Tony Cline, went down with an injury that the Lions could get a rally going. The Nittany Lions' defense led the turnaround by bottling up the Hurricanes' offense. Ham, whom Charlie hated to see on Bloody Tuesdays, was gleefully inflicting physical and emotional pain on Miami's players. Ham recovered a fumble, blocked a kick, and seemed to be playing the game with his identical twin on the field at the same time. Ham and his associates held the Miami offense to an unbelievable 20 yards in the second half.

Charlie matched Ham's energy on the offensive side of the ball. He scored all three Lions touchdowns and piled up 123 yards—all the while running from the clutches of the Stork.

After the smoke cleared on a 22–7 Penn State victory, Miami coach Charlie Tate paid Paterno's team the highest compliment a team could receive in 1968.

"This is the best team we've faced," he said. "Better than USC."

With three games remaining in the season, the Lions were ranked number three in the nation again. Of course, that meant Paterno was beside himself with worry. Overconfidence against Kansas State hadn't been a problem, but that snake could tunnel into the garden any moment.

The nation's sportswriters were enamored of Paterno's team of nonconformists. They waxed rhapsodic about the eight players who shaved their heads to create "an identity" for themselves in the plain-wrap Penn State system. They composed sonnets about Kwalick's pass-catching abilities, Onkotz's proficiency at math, and Reid's musical talents. Charlie's Heisman hype was growing and would extend into the next year, while Campbell was universally respected as a running back to be reckoned with.

Paterno worried that the players might start believing their press clippings.

What he should have counted on was a defensive unit as effective as a blackjack to the back of the head—and Charlie Pittman's abject fear of failure.

The year before, Charlie felt ashamed about his performance in his home state. Given a second chance by the providence of sport, he meant to show his family and hometown fans just how much he'd grown. And he'd give Lou Saban more reason to regret his poor choice of words when touting the Maryland program.

Maryland

Defense started the day. Smear intercepted a pass by Maryland and ran it back 40 yards for an early 7–0 lead. Fumble recoveries set up two more touchdowns, making the score 21–0 in the early going.

Charlie ran in two touchdowns, including one that caused a tackler to miss so badly, he looked as if he had simply thrown himself on the ground. Campbell and Abbey also scored touchdowns, leading to a 57–13 citrus-flavored blowout.

Its 16th straight game without a loss meant Penn State was Orange Bowl bound.

The University of Pittsburgh Panthers just happened to be in the wrong game at the wrong time. Sure the contest was in Pitt Stadium, but it had been 13 months since the Lions had lost and Pittsburgh was an in-state rival that had won eight national championships between the 1910s and 1930s. One of the sweetest phrases in all of sports is "bragging rights." The Panthers had managed just one win during the season and were 1–8 by the time Saturday, November 23, rolled around.

Pittsburgh

Against the overmatched Panthers Charlie scored three times, rarely getting roughed up by defenders. Paterno sat him and the other starters early and still he couldn't rein in the scoring. The

Lions scored 35 points in the second period alone and had a 58–9 lead by the third quarter.

"Joe was really trying to hold the score down," Charles recalls. "He hated to rub a team's face in it. He laid into Mike Cooper [a backup quarterback for throwing a touchdown pass. We understood what he was trying to do, but all year long we had been taught how to get into the end zone. Some of these guys hadn't seen any playing time and they were just doing what he taught us to do."

The Lions won their biggest blowout of the year, 65–9.

Next up?

"Oh, I couldn't wait to play Syracuse," Charles says. "I wanted to go to Syracuse and wear Jim Brown's No. 44. I later found out that they used to wave that number in front of all the running backs they recruited. But I didn't get recruited by Syracuse so I always gave a little extra effort when we played against them."

Syracuse

On the anniversary of the attack on Pearl Harbor, December 7, the Lions took on the Orangemen with two goals in mind—winning and staying healthy for their Orange Bowl engagement. The mission was accomplished with a ball control offense that watched the clock and attempted nothing tricky. Penn State won its last regular season game of 1968 by a score of 30–12.

It had been a long journey for Charlie from when he first stepped onto the field at Beaver Stadium and heard the ungodly noise of college football hits to when he became a first stringer on the number-three team in the nation. As the team prepared for its date with the University of Kansas in the Orange Bowl, Charlie was stretching on the field during a lull in practice when an epiphany took hold.

"I realized that I was better as a player because I had to face those tough defensive guys at every practice," he said. "Our opponents saw them once in a year, maybe. But our guys were great defenders and they tried their best to beat me up all season long. That made me tougher. If I hadn't been prepared for that, I would have been a totally different player and a totally different person."

From that moment, Charlie knew he would do his best never to enter a situation unprepared.

In 1991, after sitting through a redshirt freshman year, Tony was finally on the field. Although he wasn't yet playing, he was closer to his goal. The season began with seventh-ranked Lions taking on Georgia Tech at Giants Stadium. They won 34–22 and would improve on their 9–3 1990 record by going 11–2 for the year.

What Tony had waited and worked for came to pass on September 7, 1991, when Penn State played Cincinnati. It was the first home game of the season, and Tony was finally walking down the tunnel as player who had a chance to get into the game. It wasn't where he planned to be, but it was a step in the right direction.

He remembers those Saturday games, especially the moments just before heading onto the field at Beaver Stadium.

"It was totally quiet in the locker room," Tony recalls. "None of us would be saying anything. There would be 100,000 people screaming, band playing, feet stomping. No one said it, but I would think, 'We're in this war together.' The only other feeling I can imagine that's close to that sensation is war. In war, it's about life and death on the line. Football's not that serious—but it's the next closest thing. It was an unbelievable feeling.

"Then Joe would come out. We'd hold hands, say the Lord's Prayer, and he'd say, 'All right, let's go.' So we went to the tunnel leading out onto the field. He'd be standing there in the tunnel's entrance with the whole team in back of him. The crowd would be going crazy and chanting: 'Joe, Joe, Joe.' I've never felt anything like it since."

Down to Business

While being coached by Paterno, both Pittmans learned how to constructively attack fear and, in the process, accomplish progressively higher goals by making the right choices. Each has made a habit of analysis, preparation, and action. That is their path to success.

In business, as in sports, there are paths to success. There are individual moments of growth, such as when by-the-book quarterback Chuck Burkhart took the biggest gamble of his career and changed a play at the line of scrimmage in the biggest game of his career.

And there are systemic paths to success. Penn State, according to some of the most knowledgeable football analysts in the country, became a nationally successful program with its 1968 Orange Bowl win. Using a mixture of discipline, toughness, consistency, and preparedness, Joe Paterno redefined his sleepy program and created a beacon for great athletes.

"If you're talking about elite athletes, the first thing you notice about them is they have self-confidence," says Ron Bracken, award-winning sportswriter for the *Centre Daily News*. "They believe in themselves. Their attitude is, 'Go ahead and put me in the toughest situation you can…and watch me succeed.' They have the courage to do whatever it takes to meet a challenge. I think that translates well into the business world."

The Secret Is Color Coded: Blue

At Penn State they call it the Blue Line—painted grass that marks the boundaries of the football field. For our present purposes let's call it your office door, a sales call, the computer keyboard, or wherever your business is conducted. Great businesspeople, like great athletes, are diligent in preparation. And many of them fear failure. Can you imagine the reactions of those 100,000 fans if the team they were rooting for just wandered out onto the field with no preparation or practice?

A Simple Rule

Make a simple rule for yourself—don't cross your personal Blue Line until you are ready to do what it takes to succeed in your business.

That starts with preparation. What does that preparation look like for you? If you don't know the answer to that question, you haven't been paying attention. To achieve, you have to be able to measure. Period.

There's a scene in the movie *Caddyshack* that addresses the notion of competition without measurement:

> Judge Smails: "Ty, what did you shoot today?"
> Ty: "Oh, Judge, I don't keep score."
> Judge Smails: "Then how do you measure yourself with other golfers?"
> Ty: "By height."

Measure, Measure, Measure

You have to know where your Blue Line starts and ends; quantify your goal and you have a way to measure success—unless height works for you as a sole indicator.

Crossing the Blue Line means concentrating on the task at hand to the exclusion of other distractions. If you want your children to call you during the day and it's not an emergency, give them a time to call. If you're on a sales call, don't work on inventory reports. Make sure you've got that smile the client can hear in your voice. At the risk of sounding like a Zen master, concentrate on being in the moment.

Separate the Movements

Every movement should be delineated in your mind—work or non-work, Blue Line or non–Blue Line. When you are at a nonwork-related lunch, eat hearty! But when you're in the office, work hard. Star athletes—and businesspeople—don't take downs off. And the secret of their success is they always know how to find the playing field. One Minnesota-based multimillionaire who has started several companies in the billion-dollar medical devices field always finds out the birthdays of associates and is diligent about sending out well-chosen birthday, Christmas, and Hanukah greeting cards. He knows where his Blue Line is and it crosses over into what many would consider his personal life.

The man has been known to raise $8 million in funding with a single telephone call. He knows that playing successfully in his rarefied air means building business relationships on the golf course, over dinner, at galas…and through greeting cards.

Five Rules to Follow When Putting Down Your Blue Line
First Rule: Punctuality

The first Blue Line rule is punctuality. Former Penn State defensive star Lee Rubin remembers that lesson well.

"Joe used to tell us that if we were a minute late for practice or film, we had to do 120 laps," Rubin recalls. "He told us that we owed everybody—120 people a minute, not just him.

"Discipline, structure, toughness: it was how we conducted our practices and, for a lot of us, it's how we now conduct our business. I teach a Sunday school class at my church and I tell those young people that being late is a big deal. I tell them you can't leave at 7:30 and arrive at 7:30. I really believe that Joe consciously wasn't just preparing us for Saturday's game; he was preparing us for life."

Second Rule: Consistency

The second Blue Line rule is consistency. Joe Paterno simply waking up in the morning is the best example of this trait.

One of Paterno's formative moments as a young man revolved around his being misinformed (perhaps intentionally) about the appropriate attire at a party that was being thrown by his moneyed classmates.

He attended the party, and shortly after his arrival he began hearing whispers about his being underdressed—and ethnic! Paterno left with his ears burning and a promise that he would never be underdressed again. Almost the next day, Paterno adopted that staple of fashion, the navy blue blazer.

Paterno's blue blazer became an icon in Happy Valley because it was his default clothing choice—a response to a slight almost 50 years in the past. That gives insight into the mind of Paterno. He sees a problem and he seeks to eradicate it—permanently.

And most of those problems, such as how to win football games the right way, are solved. Consistency is the hallmark of the Paterno method, which has been outrageously successful in its 41 years of implementation.

Consistency is also the garden where your own outrageous success can flower.

Third Rule: Pay Attention to Details

Another deeply held belief of the Pittmans and Paterno—and Blue Line rule number three—is pay attention to details.

All three men agree that large challenges are not to be tackled whole cloth. Translated into business terms, your goal may be to get a promotion, but your actions should be to make sure your paperwork is on time and of an excellent quality and to take on projects that resulted in promotions for others.

"Take care of the little things," Paterno says often, "and the big things will take care of themselves."

But don't forget to be flexible, cautions Tony Pittman. Penn State football time schedules run like a well-oiled Swiss watch.

"But there is a problem when the routine gets busted a little bit," Tony Pittman says. "Right before the Illinois game in our undefeated year, all the power went out in the hotel we were staying in. We couldn't watch film, we couldn't have a proper team meeting—the mechanical stuff was gone!

"And when the game starts, all of a sudden we were losing. We were totally out of sorts. The bad thing with that type of consistency is that if anything interrupts it, things can fall apart. And Illinois was loving it. They were hyped. At the time we were number one or number two in the country. It was by far the most amazing game I had ever been part of it. We ended up running in a touchdown in the final seconds. The whole team was holding hands on the sideline. Without our customary preparation, we were out of our element. We had no fizz; we were totally flat. But that game showed what that team was made of. That game still stands out pretty much in Penn State lore."

Fourth Rule: Be Prepared

Blue Line rule number four is be prepared. The best commercial for being prepared is a saying the Pittmans and Paterno live by: "If you're not getting better at what you do, you're getting worse."

Write this phrase somewhere you can see it frequently—an electronic Post-it note on your computer's desktop or an actual Post-it on your actual desk.

Like many things that contribute to real success, this is a deceptively simple concept. It's so simple that many people want to exercise their options on the subject. Some people think they can coast for a day or a week with no appreciable problems. Others are enamored of their ability to "wing it when I really need to."

Don't be that person. Preparation is the tool that makes you the best in your field—nothing else will do it. Your connections may get you in the door, your talent may dazzle them for a moment or two, but business and sports success are time-intensive endeavors. By way of example, your looks may attract attention like Anna Kournikova, but if you win no majors—like Kournikova—your sports career will quickly end.

Former Olympic track and field star Carl Lewis, who held world records in the long jump and 100-meter sprint, has an interesting take on getting better versus falling back into range of the competition—the middle of the pack. It fits in the microcosm of a single race. Lewis realized that fatigue would factor in over the course of every 100-meter sprint—his goal was to slow down less than the other sprinters for the last portion of the race. Lewis's training was meant to stave off entropy. In other words, because he knew his body would slow down, he trained to make sure it didn't slow down too much.

If you haven't put in the work to achieve your goals, you will get worse at doing what you do. That is a promise the universe always keeps.

In a way, football players understand this point better than most. It is driven home forcefully on the field because when you stare across that line of scrimmage you are face to face with your challenge—and your challenge has been working out four hours a day for 365 days a year with the express purpose of pounding you into the turf.

Buddha said, "All that we are is the result of what we thought." A more practical business interpretation is, "All that we are is the result of how we prepare."

Fifth and Most Important Rule: Believe
The fifth Blue Line rule is at the heart of Penn State/Pittman/Paterno success—believe. Believing in your system requires the creation of a system that you actually use.

Tim Curley offers some advice in creating such a system. He advises that you make your system the foundation of your own personal legacy.

That is at the center of his message when he says: "Each year the incoming group has to know they have responsibility and accountability to not let the sweat and tears of previous groups end with them."

You are creating a business legacy with the phone calls you make, the clothes you wear, and the meetings you attend. If you are prepared, if you respect your personal legacy, and if you sharpen your skills—always getting better rather than worse—you will stand out in today's business climate. Paradoxically, by improving yourself individually, you will be a better team player. Remember, a chain is only as strong as its weakest link.

"When I first started as a consultant at Pricewaterhouse [in the mid-1990s]," Tony Pittman recalls, "it was a different era. The company had hired hundreds and hundreds of highly motivated, upwardly mobile people. Financially, there was enough to go around. It was just a big pie. So what you had was a bunch of smart people all doing well. Because of that, there was a lot of focus on team success. People knew they would get their success, so they were fine with making it a team thing.

"But that was during a booming market. All indicators pointed up for both individuals and for teams. The attitude was, 'Let's just enjoy this ride.' Now, with a less robust economy, people seem to be getting more and more self-oriented. And those of us who are eight or 10 years into a career sense that opportunities are fewer and farther between. There is less of a focus on team and more of a focus on what can I get for myself."

What Tony observed was more people working on ways to cut corners and slam the other guy or gal and fewer people working to improve individual skill sets. It is hard to believe in a team concept in that setting.

Success means having goals that are met (and goals that replace those goals when they are achieved). Your task with these goals is the same as an elite athlete—set goals in all the pertinent areas, practice, achieve them, and surpass them.

> **WINNING IN LIFE**
> "What defines winning? In today's business climate people can stay successful in their careers simply by

mastering the art of not having things stick to them. That's a pretty low bar. Michael Jordan would not be the legend he is if he focused on not committing fouls. In my consulting days, I worked with a company whose existence was defined by how many billable hours they had. They oversaw a project with huge problems, and they were billing millions of dollars a month. That must have seemed successful to them. But the client finally said, 'You guys are horrible. Get out.' The rules of winning and losing can be manipulated easily. What I desire is winning in a meaningful way; a way that I've defined. Because if you're not careful and aware of what you desire, you can be sucked into something very different."

—*Tony Pittman*

CHAPTER 5

Want Perfection? Practice

Tony's waiting game was trying his patience and he wasn't sure what more he could do to quell his impatience. When frustrated, he called his father. Tony advocated for a starting position in Joe's office. He spent time with his friends Phil and Lee to blow off steam. Most of all, he left it all on the field. He tackled, ran, defended passes. If the coaches asked for a lap, he gave them two.

He was doing all the right things, but he still wasn't starting. He knew his success in the West Virginia game the year before, in 1992, hadn't been a fluke. He had big-time college football skills—and a seat on the pine.

He was getting angry. Though he didn't realize it at the time, that meant Paterno's motivational magic was at work.

"In a one-on-one meeting, Joe told me he regretted not pushing for me to play more," Tony said. "He was afraid it wouldn't be seen as objective because of my father."

It was official. Tony was angry. He thought he could make it on his own without running to the well of the Pittman name, and ironically, it had become a burden.

"I sensed that as a player, and most of the time it was a motivating factor," Tony recalls. "In fact, I had what I believe to be my best game in the last regular season game I would not start as a Nittany Lion—a 38–37 miracle comeback win [on November 27] against Michigan State to end the 1993 season.

"I made a few big hits, broke up a few passes…basically played very angry. It must have worked. They handed me a blue jersey, and I never let go of it. Looking back, I think Joe knew that he had to draw that out of me. It reminds me of the same switch that flipped with [running back] Larry Johnson when he finally got a starting role at Penn State. When he got it, he ran with it and never looked back, to the tune of 2,000-plus yards his senior season. He still plays that way today."

In 1994 Tony solidified his own legacy—an iron man reputation. He would be just one of two defensive players that never missed a start that season for the Lions. By the sixth game of the 1994 season, Tony had outlasted any doubts he had about his chances; the extra year in high school and his redshirt freshman year were distant memories. He was simply focused on the game.

"Top football programs don't fall like that," fifth-year senior Tony Pittman mused to himself after five consecutive starts in the 1994 resulted in wins. "Minnesota, USC, Iowa, Rutgers, Temple." The best description of the Penn State five-game scoring spree was that the team had mown down Division 1A competition—by an average score of 52–17.

Respected Big Ten and Big East opponents were so much grass under a gasoline-powered attack that chewed up not just turf, but sky as well. Fifth-year senior quarterback Kerry Collins and junior tailback Ki-Jana Carter would combine for more than 3,200 yards passing and rushing by year's end. But the fickle finger of media still pointed to Penn State as a newcomer to the esteemed Big Ten and, despite the two national championships it won in 1982 and 1986, it was still considered an Easterner, therefore suspect.

In big-time football, where programs like USC, Miami, Texas, Michigan, Ohio State, Alabama, Michigan State, and Notre Dame have ruled the roost for decades, the eastern United States is no place to make a reputation. The South, West, and Midwest are the places to be.

Just don't bother trying to sell that snake oil to Joe Paterno.

By starting the 1994 season with five straight "mow downs," his Penn State team had garnered college football's grudging attention—even if some considered the PSU offensive juggernaut to be suspect. After all, just two years ago, the Paterno system had stumbled badly in a 7–5 season that ended with a 24–3 thumping by Stanford in the Blockbuster Bowl.

Tellingly, Paterno, a master motivator and Seer of Big Pictures, confessed that he had regrets during that mediocre season. Paterno's 1992 squad had him looking backward instead of forward. He was invoking the name of his friend and predecessor, Rip Engle, when asked about the 1992 season.

"The thing that made Rip such a great coach," Paterno told a *Sports Illustrated* reporter, "is that he never lost a squad."

Paterno swore he did just that when the Nittany Lions started out 5–0 in 1992 and then lost the next five of seven games.

He was embarrassed, and he didn't like it. So in 1993, at the age of 66, he uncorked a fountain of middle age, dashing around the practice fields in cleats and shorts as if it were 1969.

The Paterno magic flowed back in 1993. He made his usual defensive adjustments, and on offense he benched John Sacca, his quarterback from 1992, and replaced him with 6'5" 235-pound Kerry Collins after the third game of that season. The ship seemed to be righted—the Nittany Lions closed out the season with five straight wins.

Still, how real were these Nittany Lions in 1994, even with a reinvigorated Joe Paterno? It was anybody's guess after just five games.

Big Test in the Big House

The real test was soon to come. On October 15, 1994, fifth-ranked Michigan, the winningest program in college football, would host the Nittany Lions, and the momentum seemed to be on Michigan's side. They were 4–1, with the only setback being a one-point loss to Colorado. And that loss stuck in their craw. Gary Moeller's Wolverines were hungry for vindication, and Penn State looked like roadkill-to-be in their eyes.

Colorado had wounded a dangerous beast in Michigan. Quarterback Kordell Stewart threw a Hail Mary pass into the end zone that resulted in a Michael Westbrook miracle catch for a 27–26 victory.

Michigan's attitude? Unconcealed rage that a "lesser team" had won.

"[The] way Colorado acted after the game," Michigan nose tackle Tony Henderson said with disgust. "They had guys saying, 'We knew we were going to win.' Come on! We won that game. They just came in and stole it like a thief who robs your house."

On October 15, Penn State would be walking into the Big House—the country's largest football stadium—with the express intent of poking a bloody Wolverine with a stick. But anyone looking for doubt in the minds of the Nittany Lions would come away empty-handed, especially at the right cornerback position—cover corner, as insiders call it. There, in the person of Tony Pittman, confidence was high.

Tony was the smallest man on the field at 5'8" and 171 pounds. Across the field, at left cornerback, Brian Miller was an inch taller and 12 pounds heavier. Together, Tony and Miller barely outweighed junior left tackle Keith Conlin—who was 6'7" and 301 pounds. But as the singularly American phrase goes, it's not the size of the dog in the fight, it's the size of the fight in the dog.

Whether in practice or games, Tony was the dictionary definition of cornerback—one of the most athletic members of the secondary with Olympic-caliber speed. Tony's job was to intercept, at high velocity, any bodies that made it past the line and to run, stride for stride, with opponents looking to catch the ball. His business was denial—and business was good.

Cornerbacks basically face a horror story on every passing down. Those 55-yard passing plays that ESPN loves to play over and over? Those plays are knives to the hearts of cornerbacks who were outjumped, outmuscled, outrun, or outthought. Arguably, cornerbacks are the most exposed players on the field. Do their job well, and all anyone notices is that their opponent seems to be running the ball a lot. Get burned, and they are buried on the bench.

That thrill can be too much for some, but Tony thrived on it. Part of his ability to handle the pressure is genetic, but those in the know see his father's training in it as well.

Charles says, "I wanted him to understand competition. He was allowed to play anything he wanted, except for football."

What Charles wanted Tony to learn before deciding to make his own mark on the gridiron were the intricacies of competition. One of the first lessons Tony would have to learn would be that winners are marked people. Charlie knew that lesson intimately.

After he became a star at Beaver Stadium, Charlie used to return home to Baltimore and experience firsthand the jealousy that success bred among those who didn't achieve it for themselves. It seemed innocent enough; he simply agreed to play sandlot football with his buddies, as he had dozens of times before in his childhood.

He soon found that playing touch football on the fields near Appleton Street in west Baltimore was a different kind of danger than the weekly mayhem at Penn State.

"Somebody was always looking to make a reputation for himself by showing you up," the elder Pittman recalls. "Anything could happen. So I always played center—unless we started losing. You could wind up with a broken collarbone playing sandlot football. I learned to stop playing sandlot football pretty fast."

Charles knew Tony's success would forever be linked to his own, and since that was unavoidable he prepared his eldest son early on. "Focus on your goal," Charles Pittman told Tony—sometimes he would say it with tenderness, sometimes as a challenge. "Focus on your goal."

Those four words were an ingenious incentive for young Tony, who, like most children, knew little about competition.

By focusing on his personal goals, there was no comparison—in Tony's mind, at least—between Charlie and Tony. No scoring championship to tear asunder father and son's bond, no neighborhood tough guy would be ripping Tony's body apart for the benefit of some cute girl on the sidelines.

Charles toughened up his grade-school age son by enlisting the aid of his nephew, Jonathan, who was several years older, heavier, stronger, and a successful athlete in his own right.

Charles wanted Jonathan to push Tony to his physical limit: play basketball with him until he could barely stand; engage him in footraces until he was out of breath. The mission was to elbow, push, and tug Tony into a realization that competition required effort and concentration.

"And I asked Jonathan to let Tony win," Charles says. "I needed Tony to experience success early. He had to work for it, but he would win if he worked hard and I wanted him to make that connection."

The connection was made.

Tony's goal was to be a student-athlete at the same high level as his father. Years of bitty basketball and youth soccer would lead to two major decisions by the Pittman family in an effort to achieve that goal. One was to allow Tony to play football as a ninth grader, and the second was to send him away to school.

Charles and Mauresé Pittman agonized over that decision. For the Pittmans, family was watched over, protected, and supported. Letting a youngster go into the world without constant supervision was not a decision entered into lightly. But in the executive boardrooms of Charles's world, he noticed young up-and-comers, the children of executives, who had gone to the nation's most prestigious boarding schools.

Charles knew that Tony, who had always displayed curiosity and a fierce intellect, would have a career in these same boardrooms in a generation or so. His goal was to make the transition from athlete to businessperson as smooth as possible for his son.

The Pittmans chose to send Tony to Phillips Academy in Andover, Massachusetts, at the start of what would have been his 12th-grade year. He reclassified as a junior and stayed two years. After Tony's success at the school, they also sent Tony's two sisters, Mauresa and Kira.

Phillips Academy is one of the most prestigious prep schools in the nation. It is an institution with rigorous academic standards and broad lawns that was founded two years after the signing of the Declaration of Independence; the school has graduated two American presidents—George H.W. Bush and George W. Bush—and four Medal of Honor recipients.

On a blustery November day in 1989, the elder President Bush took time in his speech to the school's board of trustees to praise the captain of the football team—senior Tony Pittman.

"I want to show him off to you guys that came here with me," Bush said that day. "[He's] small but fast—tough."

Five years later, Tony would need that toughness against fifth-ranked Michigan. He was the cover corner and Amani Toomer, a sleek, 6'3" 200-pound junior split end, had spent 1994 making secondaries look foolish. Boston College, Notre Dame, Iowa, and Michigan State had all been pressed by his skills and lost.

In 1993, despite holding an early 10-point lead over Michigan, Penn State had lost 21–13. The goal was not to let that happen again.

It was an overcast fall day when Tony and his teammates lined up across from Michigan. The largest college football crowd of the year had showed up at the stadium wearing the Maize and Gold school colors.

In the belly of the beast, the Nittany Lions played an inspired game. They led 16–3 at halftime. During the game, Tony discovered the constant companion of elite football players: pain. The cumulative effect of starting for those five wins meant Tony's ribs were sore. And so were his legs, his ankles, and his arms. Every sprint meant first hurdling a knife-sharp ache. Even motionless, there was a dull throb that had to be ignored.

"It was my most difficult game," he recalls. "We were on the road playing Michigan and everyone knew it was a turning point—to show you can beat Michigan on the road. And the year before, we had beaten everyone but Michigan and Ohio State."

After halftime, Michigan roared back like the powerhouse it was. Running back Tyrone Wheatley ran for two electrifying gains of 67 and 21 yards that helped put Michigan ahead 17–16. After exchanging scores with Michigan, Penn State hit back hard with a touchdown from Collins to split end Bobby Engram that exposed a soft Michigan zone.

The score was 31–24 in favor of Penn State, with 2:53 remaining in the game. More than 106,000 people let loose with a full-throated roar.

A touchdown and a two-point conversion would win it for Michigan. Adding spice to those nearly three minutes of play was the fact that number-one ranked Florida had lost that afternoon. If Michigan or Penn State won, there would be a chance the victor would replace the Gators at the top.

At cover corner, Tony felt as if he were standing nude on that long-ago Phillips Academy podium next to President Bush. Exposed—in front of 106,000 people who were fervently praying that he would fall flat on his face.

Everyone in the stadium knew Michigan would throw to Toomer at least once during the series, and it was up to Tony and his secondary mates to stop him.

Now the game had gone beyond pain. Physical ability was a reference point. What it came down to in that moment was simple—heart. Who wanted to win more?

Michigan quarterback Todd Collins took the snap and linemen from both teams crashed into each other, the hands of a crazy, clapping giant. Toomer was gliding up the field with his sprinter's gait and Tony was in motion. For a moment, the pain was gone and he was in full stride, ready for the strike that could be a beginning or an end to the season.

Todd Collins threw a bomb toward Toomer and everyone in the stadium held a collective breath. It looked like he would catch it.

Father and son posed for Nittany Lions football cards some 25 years apart, Charlie (top) in 1969, and his son Tony in 1994.

Halfback Charlie Pittman slashed through opposing defenses from 1967 to 1969, earning All-America honors as a senior.

Pittman's 2,236 career rushing yards landed him in the top 10 of Penn State's all-time list, in the company of Lydell Mitchell, Curt Warner, John Cappelletti, and other Nittany Lion legends.

Joe Paterno, who would be a coaching legend by the time Charlie Pittman's son Tony arrived on campus, was only in his second year when the senior Pittman debuted in 1967.

The coach enjoyed many moments like this one during Charlie Pittman's college career, posting consecutive 11–0 seasons in 1968 and 1969.

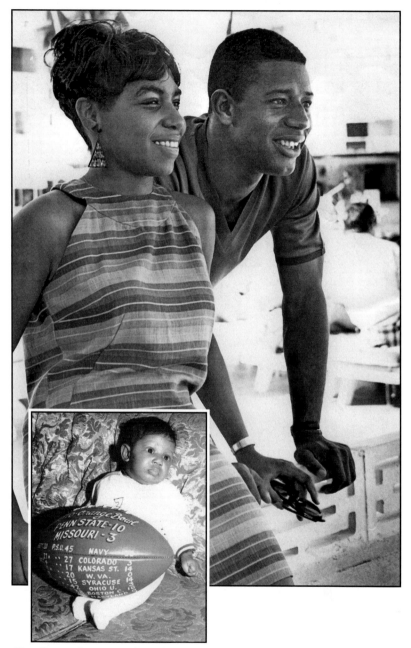

Charlie and Mauresé took time out to see the sights of Miami
prior to the 1970 Orange Bowl, which was a 10–3 victory
over Missouri, as learned early in life by young Tony (inset).

Tony Pittman was a starting cornerback on the 1994 team that, like his father's teams in '68 and '69, went undefeated but was denied a national championship because of the imprecision of the poll system.

Though the hair is a little grayer than it was during his father's era (top), the Joe Paterno that Tony Pittman played for in 1994 still employed his trademark cuffed trousers. *Photo courtesy of AP/Wide World Photos*.

Charles Pittman poses with his family, clockwise from his left, wife Mauresé, daughter Mauresa, daughter-in-law Tega, daughter Kira, and son Tony.

Tony poses with his wife Tega at the 1995 Rose Bowl. They are now the proud parents of daughter Isabella and son Anthony Charles (pictured), who in 2024 may become the third generation of Penn State Pittmans to wear No. 24.

Stopping Toomer meant the team was one step closer to the season's goal. Not making the play would mean that another route to that goal had to be found. Paterno was screaming on the sideline, his attentive eye recognizing a mistake on the defensive coverage.

"In tough fights, you have to have a short memory," Tony says. "Just like life in the business world. You don't have a lot of time to lick your wounds. If that key presentation to the boss doesn't go well, what are you going to do? You'd better start preparing for that next opportunity."

With a last-second burst of speed, Tony rushed to jam the play.

But amazing athlete that he was, Toomer caught it, despite being sandwiched between Tony and strong safety Jason Collins. Collins and Tony collided and Toomer ended up on the ground with the ball.

On the next play, Tony literally gritted his teeth. Sweat was pouring into his eyes.

"They got that one, and that's it. No more," Tony muttered to himself.

With every down an Armageddon, Tony and his defensive mates kept at it, fighting until the last whistle—and the eventual win. Against one of the most high-powered offenses in college football history, he and his defensive teammates took pride in preserving a crucial win. And for the first time in years, Penn State would be ranked number one in the nation.

As the sun rose in Happy Valley on November 15, 1969, Joe Paterno was restless. He'd been up for hours busily reviewing the day's game plan for the Maryland Terrapins. His eraser was in death throes from a furious workout, and Paterno still wasn't satisfied. It wasn't the schemes or the personnel he really wanted to take his eraser to, it was the calendar. He wanted to erase that gap in the calendar without a game. His team, unbeaten in 26 games, had been off for two weeks and hadn't played a game in Beaver Stadium for three weeks.

The 20-minute walk to the stadium simply gave him more time to fret; he walked briskly, oblivious to the fall chill. Twenty-six victories were plenty of wins for a bunch of young men; it might make them feel entitled and vulnerable to a hard shot to the head from the Terrapins.

Ever the master strategist, Paterno floated his concerns to the sportswriters who telephoned and hovered; Paterno knew full well his motley crew of eggheads and voracious readers would pick up on his words.

"Heck," he said to an assistant. "I'm just going to keep my fingers crossed."

Charlie was dealing with a different emotion—elation. The two-week break had been just what the doctor ordered. His badly aching right ankle felt the best it had since the opening seconds of the Colorado game, when a Buffalo player in a pileup mistook it for a combination lock. Charlie's energy had been contagious. That Friday's bull session with fellow running backs Lydell Mitchell and Franco Harris was a great way to let off steam: laughing, playing cards, and boasting about who was going to do what against those poor Maryland guys, Charlie's homeboys.

Harris and Mitchell always liked it when Charlie cut loose.

"Oh, my goodness," Mitchell recalls. "Charlie was such a church-going kid. He was two years ahead of me and a great ballplayer, but me and Franco called him a square."

To this day, Mitchell appreciates Charlie's support.

"Number one, there weren't many of us up there and especially not that many black athletes," Mitchell says. "When you looked at the numbers, there were 10, maybe 12 guys. That was plenty for schools at the time. On the rest of the campus there were only 300 black students in a school of 25,000. We had to stick together.

"It helped that we liked each other. We used to play card games and we'd talk about a number of things. Franco and I looked at him as our mentor. We learned so much from him, not only about football. He was experienced about things in general and he was a lot more comfortable about things on campus than we were. He knew where we could go and kind of stay out of trouble.

"We'd go to The Creamery to get ice cream; we'd hang out on the corners downtown, or the drug store on Cunningham watching cars go by, or go eat late at night. There wasn't a lot to do at Penn State back then. But after a while, we had the ability to do a little more that what Charlie showed us. We would go to parties; drink beer. Charlie didn't drink. I believe he tried to set an example for us whenever we went someplace together. Charlie and his roommate, Jim Kates, were quite a bit more reserved than Franco and me."

It was a source of great mirth for the younger Harris and Mitchell that, after a big game, Charlie eschewed wine, women, and song, and indulged his sweet tooth. They joked that if the team won a national championship, Charlie's beverage of choice would be chocolate milk instead of champagne.

Still, it was Pittman's polished demeanor that would calm things down both in pressure-cooker game situations and in the gray corners of the alien, predominantly white Happy Valley community to which they had all been transplanted.

But on the eve of the Maryland game, Charlie was boisterous and nearly as loud as Mitchell and Harris.

Against Maryland, the church kid let loose. In an offensive display that startled even the seasoned Paterno, he rushed for three touchdowns in a 10-minute span. The game was never in doubt because defensive stalwarts Onkotz, Ham, Reid, and Smear—the Rover Boys—were locking down their opponents' offensive scheme.

The hyperactive Ham set up Charlie's first score by blocking a Terrapins' punt at the 33-yard line. Reid set up his third touchdown by tipping a pass into the hands of Lions' teammate Paul Johnson.

Defensive captains Smear and Reid earned reputations in their sophomore year for being fast, aggressive, and vengeful. When

Charlie went down in the season's second game against Colorado, the two chatted on the sidelines like a surly Alphonse and Gaston.

"[Colorado quarterback] Bob Anderson is all mine now," Reid said to Smear.

"If you don't get him, I will," Smear replied.

Against Maryland, every time Charlie or any other member of the offense scored, it was a personal challenge for the defensive squad to stop a Terrapins drive. The only drawback in their eyes was they couldn't push the Maryland score into negative digits.

Charlie repeatedly slapped the shoulder pads of the Rover Boys and the drum-tight offensive line of Tom Jackson, Bob Holuba, Warren Koegel, Charlie Zapiec, and Vic Surma. Both units were playing an inspired game. There was more to come. Fans applauded crazily in the second quarter when Reid intercepted a pass and returned it 26 yards for his first college touchdown.

As he prowled the sidelines in the fourth quarter, looking for substitutes for his starters, Paterno allowed himself a smile. Twenty-seven wins in a row. Who'd a thunk it?

Charlie wasn't thinking numbers as the teams shook hands, though he would later realize he had scored the 26th touchdown of his career. His thoughts were consumed by the prospect of a double-scoop ice cream cone from The Creamery—maybe a triple—as he trotted to the locker room.

"Good game, Charlie!" Paterno called out.

"Thanks, Joe!" he called back. Walking back through the tunnel, he locked eyes with Franco and Lydell—and they all burst out laughing. Charlie deserved his chocolate-chip treat and the teasing sure to come from Franco and Lydell.

Even across the years, Tony and Charlie shared the Penn State tradition of exhaustive preparation.

"My father always taught me to focus on my goals, and that was helpful when I got to Penn State. He said it wouldn't be easy and it wasn't. But I had already encountered some situations where I had to work hard to achieve a goal on the field. While I was at Andover, the preseason conditioning packet given to the skill players had a typo in it," Tony says. "It said we were supposed to be able to run six laps in 12 minutes or less. It was supposed to read 'seven laps.' I found out about the typo pretty late and I literally was at the track the next day because I had just made it in six laps. I kept at it; I had to. I had left home, gone to boarding school for this, and it was either make the time or not be on the team. It was a heck of a lot of pressure for a kid. I finally ran it in less than the allotted time. I don't want to sound like a Nike commercial, but if you want it, you've got to just do it."

Tony and Charles say the teamwork on the field was mirrored by the tireless work of the assistant coaches. Tony fondly remembers several of those assistants from his years in the program.

He said, "You dealt with the assistant coaches much more than Joe. My position coaches, of course, I spent a great deal of time with. There were other coaches who were amazing people that stick out in my mind, even now. All the assistants left their mark on you."

Ron Dickerson—"He was one of my position coaches. He was there just for my first year. He left to become defensive coordinator at Clemson, and later, Temple's head coach. I didn't come to Penn State as a defensive back. I was mainly an offensive player in high school. He taught me the most, since I started from zero."

Greg Schiano—"After Ron left, Greg took over as defensive backs coach. Anyone following college football these days knows the amazing turnaround that Greg has orchestrated at Rutgers as its head coach. I can say that it all started when he got promoted from graduate assistant to position coach under Joe Paterno. Greg and I didn't always see eye to eye. But I'm pretty confident that we can both look back on those years as critical to the success we enjoy today. Greg really was the one who taught me how to play defense."

Tom Bradley—"They called him Scrap. He played at Penn State as a special teams player and was a special teams coach when I was there. He didn't coach my position, but I still talk to him whenever I go back. He was always one to joke and lighten things up a little bit. He considered my father to be his idol. I think he kept a watchful eye out on me."

Fran Gantner—"He was a great guy to have around. I spent most of my practices playing against his teams. A guy like him, having been around for years and basically seen it all, he was good at being prepared for the craziest things. He had a calming presence that was kind of contagious. One of my good friends, Phil Collins, and I used to talk about how much influence Fran had on the team's personality."

Kenny Jackson—"Kenny was an All-American receiver on the '82 team and went on to play with the Philadelphia Eagles for a number of years. We lost five games one year after Kenny had finished playing in the pros and he wanted to come back and help the team. He probably made the biggest difference because he was such a breath of fresh air. He coached the wide receivers, but he influenced the whole team. He was a very confident guy—loud, boisterous. And he appreciated great plays on either side of the ball. I remember against Michigan State, I nailed a guy on the flat and on the film of the play, you can see Kenny jumping five feet straight in the air. I'll go on record and say I don't know if we would have gone undefeated without him. I was sad to see him leave the staff."

Jim Caldwell—"Jim Caldwell was a great coach. He went on to coach Wake Forest and then went with Tony Dungy to Tampa Bay and now he's with Tony Dungy in Indianapolis. He was a great guy to be around. Jim is black and when my girlfriend—who's now my wife—asked me where she could go to get her hair done, I talked to Jim. Now it's great to see that he finally got a Super Bowl ring with the Colts."

Joe Sarra—"He retired a year or so ago. He coached a lot of great linebackers, guys like Andre Collins."

"So many of those coaches, I see them and they're like part of my family," Tony says. "They were tough, don't get me wrong, but they were there for you. They sincerely looked to help all the players."

A Peek Behind the Curtain

"My father taught me that whenever we were doing any conditioning drills my goal was to finish wherever the top guy finished— until I was the top guy," Tony says. "Early on, you hitch yourself to him and don't give him an obvious reason for him to think he's better than you. That's what I tried to do. During my early years in the secondary, I watched Leonard Humphries, how he practiced, what he did. That's the standard. If you want to be rich, emulate people who are wealthy and then elevate it and make it your own.

"Coming through the Penn State system taught me about setting a standard for myself based on demonstrated success. It was never about achieving certain statistics. My goal was to be as good a player as whoever was the best out there."

To achieve that goal, both Charlie and Tony had to practice long, painful hours. Nothing happens in a football game without practice.

It's safe to say that the three hours a college team spends playing an actual game is supported by literally thousands of hours of practice and preparation. While staying in shape is a year-round task, getting into a football mind-set begins a month before a season's first game. Then the players practice twice a day, the first two days without pads. Usually, two scrimmages are held to get the players' minds into real game mind-sets.

"The misconception a lot of people have is college football players only spend a lot of time lifting weights and running around," Tony says. "We spent a lot of time in a classroom setting usually from 2:30 [PM] to 4:30 [PM] learning stuff. More than half the time a football player spends getting ready for a game is dedicated to cerebral pursuits—studying film, sitting in meetings, going over plays."

It was when they were finally on the practice field that the Pittmans got their clearest glimpse of Paterno. Tony was always amused by Paterno's obsession with unusual time increments when the Lions were being put through their paces on the practice field.

"Joe used to tweak things down to the minute. He'd tell the whole squad, I'm going to add one minute and 30 seconds or take away two minutes and 15 seconds," Tony recalls. "I don't know if he really thought it made a difference. I think it was his way of sending a signal of how slim the difference was between winning and losing. He'd stand in front and say he was adjusting by a minute here, a minute there. I know people asked him about that, but he's the type of magician who never gives up the secrets to his tricks."

Charles Pittman agrees.

He said, "He ran his practices on a tight timeframe and it was always some weird number that he was focused on; I think it was his way of making us pay attention to detail—keeping us aware of time and focused."

Paterno's practice routines in the early 1990s were basically unchanged from the 1960s. Players came in for preseason precision workouts. When the players were at home, the football department sent them cards that spelled out the conditioning expectations for the upcoming preseason workouts.

"The cards said, here's what you need to do; here's what you should be able to do," Charles says. "That's how they kept us in shape and ready, with those prescribed workouts. Every player had to send the card back to let the coaches know he could do those things. They didn't take your word for it. They tested you to make sure you could do them. If you couldn't do what they asked, you couldn't come to camp."

Charlie reveled in the mental game of football.

"I was unhappy with myself if I felt like I couldn't give a full effort," he says. "I paid close attention to details. I considered myself a cerebral player. It never took me much time to learn a play. I knew where every lineman was supposed to be; I knew who the key hitters were on defense; I knew who to avoid."

It's an interesting twist of fate that Tony and Charlie were on opposite sides of the ball, yet still hated many of the same drills.

"They'd tell the defensive backs to come over and they'd bring in the fullbacks," Tony remembers. "More than once I ended up going against [5′11″, 227-pound] Sam Gash. One of the drills I feared the most was when they set up cones about five yards apart and the goal was for the fullback to go from one end to the other. They'd just pitch him the ball and say, 'Go!'"

This was one of the drills that Charlie dreaded on Bloody Tuesdays of yore.

"The guy's not going to make a move," Tony says. "He's going to try and run you over. We had a lot of those tough drills. As defensive backs, coverage was one thing—we had to prevent the big offensive pass play—but we also had to be able to tackle. My tactic was just to get a hold on the guy. I didn't try to deliver a death blow. It was technical: make contact, grab on, and don't let go. You're not going to be able to survive very long if you're giving up your body on every hit."

Another drill that tested the defensive backs' talents to their limits was one-on-one pass coverage.

"Joe would blow his whistle and shout for us to line up for one-on-ones," Tony says. "He'd bring over the quarterbacks and the wide receivers. It was just you and the wide out—no pass rush. It's tough to win the majority of those battles. Joe would put you in situations that were much more difficult than the actual games. I figured if I could succeed half the time, I'd do great in the games."

Both men—like their teammates—also had to find time to do well in their schoolwork.

"Especially in-season, it's rough scheduling classes," Tony says. "You pretty much have to schedule classes in the morning—I always had 8:00 AM classes. The reason is you wanted to get done by 1:00 PM. Then you headed to the practice field, wait in the tape line, talk with trainers, meet with your position coaches. From the start at 2:30 to getting changed, meeting, practice, and getting showered and out, you're looking at 7:30 or 8:30 before you were done.

"I learned to compartmentalize what we had to get done in that four-hour period [of in-season practice]. You don't make it if you don't rid your mind of distractions. Then, after practice is done, you go back to being a college student."

| **Down to Business** | Focus on your goal. This is one of the trickiest concepts to translate from sports to business. "Focus on your goal" can mean so many things in both endeavors. The reason for the difficulty is the same in sports and business—it's hard to extricate personal goals from team goals. |

Individual or Collective?

For example, your personal income is affected by your business's revenues, but which is more important? After all, this is the 21st century; your company loyalty may be met with downsizing. Or shareholders may get dividends while you get pay freezes.

It's an executive decision and you need to make it. Is your goal an individual or collective goal?

After making your executive decision, your initial step in focusing on your goal is to precisely and specifically define your goal. Don't be shy about it if it's purely financial. If that is so, set your salary goals for the year. If it's advancement, set a year's time-frame for moving up within your organization. If it's some other measurement—recognition, awards, job satisfaction—quantify it and set a target date.

"If you can't measure it; you can't manage it," says Charles Pittman. "You get what you inspect, not what you expect."

Penn State Two-Step

It's a Penn State two-step, Pittman-style. First, recognize the goal. Second, set a deadline for achievement.

In football, unlike many business situations, the season is already set for the team. Everyone knows the Saturday regular season itineraries—that's taken care of by schedulers.

So Penn State does what all elite sports teams do: concentrate on achieving every goal that would lead them to their ultimate goal of a national championship. That is a collective goal, by the way.

The secret to achieving goals is to attain a level of sophistication about the steps needed to accomplish that goal. A quick digression: America and Great Britain have the world's two most overweight populations because losing weight requires a multipartite solution—restraint, exercise, and constant achievement of weight-loss goals. Achieving such a complicated goal requires sophistication beyond, "I need to lose 10 pounds."

Tony, and every teammate of his, knew that national champions generally have one or no losses in the course of a season. That translates to no more than one loss as a goal. It's quantifiable.

The steps to achieving that goal meant all the usual things—working out, learning the playbook, studying the opponents. Things you should also be doing in your business.

Pace Yourself

It also meant knowing which games would be more difficult tests and doing whatever it took to meet those challenges.

In the business world, too many are oblivious to the serious losses they incur in a workday. Failing to meet a sales goal might not be as fatal as being stuck with a nickname that saps the respect of your coworkers, thereby thwarting your advancement hopes.

For the 1994 Nittany Lions, Michigan was a red-letter date for two very important reasons; it represented the sixth game of the season. And in the sixth games of the 1992 and 1993 seasons, Penn State lost, and in one case, went on a losing spiral.

And of course, it was Michigan, one of the strongest programs in college football history.

Knowing that the season's goal could be lost on the field at Michigan, Tony knew he had to be ready. Despite being battered and in pain, he did two things: he focused and he prepared.

On the pass play to Toomer there was no crowd noise in Tony's mind. Certainly, there was nervousness and even a mistake in coverage. But there would be no second-guessing the outcome. Tony and his teammates expected to meet their challenges and win.

That is how your business goals will present themselves—a series of challenges that are either met or unmet.

Focus on your goal—and turn to the next chapter.

WINNING IN LIFE

"I think too many managers focus in on their employees' weaknesses. To me that's like faulting Shaquille O'Neal for not shooting the three-point shot well. I believe you should make your strengths as strong as possible. In business, check your employees' track records. Find out what they're good at. For example, many good salespeople are not very organized. Why waste time insisting they get organized? Hire an assistant. Why waste your time trying to turn a strength into a weakness?"

—Charles Pittman

CHAPTER 6

The Team Comes First

B oston College, West Virginia, Syracuse, Maryland, North Carolina State, Ohio, Pittsburgh, Florida State (tie), Navy, Kansas State, West Virginia, UCLA, Boston College, Army, Miami, Maryland, Pittsburgh, Syracuse, Kansas, Navy, Colorado, Kansas State, West Virginia, Syracuse, Ohio, Boston College, Maryland, Pittsburgh, North Carolina State, Missouri, West Virginia, Pittsburgh, Minnesota, USC, Iowa, Rutgers, Temple, Michigan, Ohio State, Indiana, Illinois, Northwestern, Michigan State, Oregon—these teams comprise the 44 victories and one tie of the Pittman Eras at Penn State. Each of them was a drama played out on a 360' × 160' stage; a series of intimate passion plays for 100,000 friends. And each of these victories underscored a concept that a remarkable number of successful businesspeople have internalized: the team comes first.

With the possible exception of the Orange Bowl tie with Florida State, Penn State fans were satisfied every time Charlie or Tony started a game for Paterno.

With each sprint onto the field, whether to the jet-engine-loud adulation at Beaver Stadium or the raucous shouts and boos at Michigan, they were humbled. Both Charlie—the scion of a poor family, a young man who never dreamed he possessed something so valuable it would put him on such a grand stage—and Tony—who grew up sheltered in a well-to-do family and had to push his natural talents to the limit to achieve that stage—were awed by the spectacle.

Both of them knew success was impossible without those 99 other blue-and-white-clad guys and their coaching and support staff. Football reinforces the concept of team like few other sports.

"We're building a tradition here," Paterno would say. Frequently he would add, "Take care of the little things and the big things will take care of themselves."

Nearby, a few of the senior football players rolled their eyes, having heard this many times before.

The magic of the homily about taking care of the little things is not so much in its repetition—and it is one of Paterno's favorites—but in Paterno's gift for making it real in the eyes of impressionable teenagers and young adults. In his raspy voice, the well-worn phrase eventually becomes an amino acid, a building block of life for motivated young men like the Pittmans.

Penn State's football program takes care of the little things. Under Paterno, it is nearly militaristic in the level of its structure. For example, whether the Lions played home or away, everyone was taken off to a hotel the day before a game. Distractions were not to be tolerated. Friday was a day to think purely of football and one's individual role on the team.

Players and staff were issued laminated cards and those cards were miniature bibles for the day leading up to a particular game. Each card was the harried result of countless hours of support staff work; the cards bore instructions, step by step and minute by minute, as to what the possessor of the card was to be doing to prepare for the game. Consider it an exceedingly bossy Visa card. Time was allotted for meals, the team prayer, watching film, and Joe's speech. Paterno masterfully articulated his expectations in person and the cards were touchstones for that eloquence.

And in that wondrous sleight of hand of his, he was teaching a lesson with the cards; it was a small thing that lead up to a big thing—the week's opponent.

In the vernacular of sports, Paterno would never be a coach who "rolls out the balls and lets 'em play." He knew too much about the millions of things that can go wrong between practice and games. Legendary U.S. general George S. Patton once noted that an army travels on its stomach—a nod to the reality that food and other support supplies are just as important to soldiers as rifles.

A football team is a big hungry beast, too. It requires food, land, clothing, and direction. It is made up of big hungry kids who each need the same things, with another 100,000 needs and wants thrown in for good measure. A football team can have injured stars, rising second stringers, disgruntled benchwarmers, arrogant freshmen, and bewildered seniors all in the same whirlpool bath.

The size of the teams and the array of situations requiring one to trust others are central to football's mystique as a game and way of life. How important is teamwork in football? In a 2005 game against Wisconsin, quarterback Michael Robinson was blasted by Wisconsin's hulking defensive end Erasmus James. Robinson lay on the ground at Beaver Stadium for several long minutes and had to be taken to a hospital. Days later, when word got to James that Robinson's mother wished someone would tackle James that hard, he responded: "What she should wish for is a better offensive line for her son."

Flashback to October 29, 1994, and Tony Pittman discovering the importance of teamwork for himself.

They Beat Ohio State By How Much?

There are 97,079 fans crammed into Beaver Stadium and most can't believe what they're seeing. Fourteenth-ranked Ohio State— yes, that Ohio State—is being steamrolled by Penn State offensively and defensively.

A newcomer to rough and tumble Big Ten football, no one knew how long it would be before Penn State rose to an elite level in the conference. On this particular Saturday, just one year after joining the Big Ten, the answer is: not long.

Looking up into the stands, something he rarely makes time for in most contests, Tony sees the crowd going nuts and sending their digits into the late afternoon chill.

"We're number one!"

He allows himself a smile beneath his plain white helmet, wipes his hands on his blue jersey, and readies himself for the next series of downs.

He curls his lips into a frown; it's back to business as he hears the defensive scheme being barked out. He has to return to that quiet place in his mind where his concentration is nearly total.

As with his other starts, Tony's personal pregame ritual was to watch a college football game. Preparing for a game that way is like immersing himself in a lake on a warm summer day. The collisions on the small tube are soothing; they calm him and cleanse away the extraneous thoughts. His objective is to have his body on the field but his mind, sharp and dispassionate, in the broadcast booth of his thoughts.

"Just do the job," he murmurs just as the ball is snapped.

A precise player, Tony likes playing the angles so beloved by his coach. And those angles are working like magic this afternoon against the Buckeyes.

Though he might be outsized by some of the best college receivers in the nation, he is determined never to be outthought.

In the back of his mind, Tony kept a three-year-old recording of Paterno's screaming voice from a game he hadn't started. It was October 12, 1991, and the Lions were playing Miami.

"Miami was number two in the country and it was a close game, a game of inches. The Hurricanes had a long punt return and followed that up with another long play," Tony recalls. "Leonard Humphries was playing [left cornerback] and he was supposed to be six yards deep on the play. He lined up at five and three-quarter yards and got beat by a quarter yard. Joe just lit into him on the sidelines, ate him alive. That was Joe's mentality. If he'd been one foot deeper, he would have made that play. More often than not, he was right."

Those few inches are tremendously important on October 29. Penn State is the number one team in the nation. Three yards and a cloud of dust? Not this version of the Lions. Offensive coordinator Fran Gantner, Paterno's right-hand man and friend of some 30 years, has supercharged the reliable Penn State offense. This is a high-scoring team with two legitimate Heisman Trophy candidates: quarterback Kerry Collins and tailback Ki-Jana Carter. Collins and Carter are posting such ridiculously gaudy offensive numbers they probably canceled each other out in the Heisman vote.

By the end of the 1994 season, Penn State would lead the nation with an offensive output of 520.2 yards per game, set 14 team school records, 19 individual school marks, and two Big Ten marks. The Lions' 48.1 points per game would set a Big Ten record for average points per game.

Tony knows what his team is capable of this afternoon, but he has to keep his attention on Ohio State junior quarterback Bobby Hoying to make sure he and his receivers don't start making big plays.

Still, it is Halloween weekend in Happy Valley and the crowd noise is unabated, a continuous ovation that spikes with each touchdown, interception, or tackle for a loss.

Athletes occasionally speak of the zone, a magical, athletic place where the physically gifted see everything, except themselves, moving in slow motion. In the zone, an athlete can snatch a fly out of the air or grab a quarter from the top of goalpost and leave 15 cents change.

"It just clicked," Tony recalls years later. "It took two or three years, but by that time, all the wacky sounding defensive calls were second nature. I knew what was happening on the field and the scheme felt natural. It just seemed like I knew what they were going to do and I didn't have to think about it."

Tony was in the zone and in full denial mode. By game's end, both defense and offense had displayed complete mastery of the Buckeyes, as evidenced by the 63–14 score.

"We knew we were good right then and there," Tony recalls.

With their domination of the 21st-ranked team in the nation, coming just two weeks after manhandling 15th-ranked Michigan, Penn State players and coaches were ready for another week at number one in the country. They were half right.

The team remained number one in the *USA Today/CNN* poll, but dropped to number two in the Associated Press poll. Nebraska, which had been number three, leapfrogged over Penn State to take the number one AP spot.

Penn State linebacker Willie Smith was livid; his slam of the AP pollsters was quoted in *Sports Illustrated* magazine.

"We dropped?" he screamed in the locker room. "Sixty-three to 14 and we dropped! What do they want us to do to these teams?"

Paterno, who knows a little something about fickle polls, counseled his players to keep their concentration and close out the season. Game eight against Indiana would be a milestone, and if they played their hand properly, a national championship still looked achievable.

But the troika of games—Ohio State, Indiana, Illinois—would provide some of the strangest football moments in Penn State history.

Joe's Gallantry Bites Lions in Heinie

The Indiana game, played in Bloomington, was nearly as one-sided as the Ohio State affair in terms of Penn State domination. The Lions led by three touchdowns in the fourth quarter. The Hoosiers, never a traditional football power, were a safe team for a coach to call off the dogs. Paterno never believed in running up a score against an overmatched opponent.

That chivalry would come back to bite Paterno and his team on the hindquarters. Paterno rested Tony and the other starters to give game experience to second-string players. When Indiana got the football, the Hoosiers scored a late game touchdown against the Nittany Lions' reserves. When the second unit Penn State offense didn't close out the game, Indiana got the football back once again.

The Hoosiers scored on a Hail Mary fling into the end zone and then Coach Bill Mallory called for a two-point conversion. That successful play made the final score 35–29.

The team trotted off the field with an 8–0 record, smiles on their faces and visions of again being the number one undisputed team in America dancing in their heads.

A strange thing happened on the way to number one, though. The sportswriters who voted on the poll didn't get the directions.

It should be noted that modern football, like modern business, often has its bottom line affected by global forces beyond its control. Sometimes making the best mousetrap gets you the same response as a convincing gridiron win—much less than expected.

Nebraska was now number one in both polls.

There were several factors in the odd reaction of the polls to Penn State's perfect record. Some said the win over Indiana wasn't convincing—ignoring the fact Paterno played his second unit for much of the last quarter. Some said Nebraska's two most recent wins, 45–17 over Kansas and 24–7 over number two Colorado, offered compelling evidence of a number one team.

But football insiders suspected an off-the-field influence—the Osborne Factor. Tom Osborne, coach of the Nebraska Cornhuskers, was a well-respected coach from a well-respected football region who had never won a national championship. He was nearing retirement, and for him to leave the game without a championship just seemed wrong.

Many sportswriters felt Osborne's 1981, 1983, and 1993 teams all should have won the top honor. Especially egregious in their eyes was the fate of his 1983 Cornhuskers. That team was considered one of the best college football teams ever. Nebraska went 12–0 during the regular season, never slipping from number one, and was a favorite to win the 1984 Orange Bowl against number five Miami.

In a nail biter of a game, Nebraska scored a late touchdown against Miami to get within one point, 31–30. But in a gutsy move,

Osborne ordered his team to try for a two-point conversion in the final seconds. An extra-point kick—almost automatic in college football—would have led to a tie, overtime, and probably a national championship for Nebraska, but Osborne believed in his team. The two-point conversion attempt failed, giving Miami the victory and the 1983 national title.

Osborne became a rock star to sportswriters across the nation. He was a guy with moxie.

But the Penn State defense couldn't tackle Tom Osborne's legend. All Tony and the Lions could do was beat the teams that took the field against them.

They were shocked to see they had dropped a notch to number two in the polls after their Halloween massacre of Ohio State.

The next game at Illinois was a gut check for the team.

A Broken Routine—and Cold Pizza

Besides being slighted by the polls, fate provided an ill-timed power outage for the Nittany Lions. The day before the game against the Fighting Illini in Champaign-Urbana, the high-rise hotel where the Lions were staying lost its power.

Here is a poorly kept secret: Paterno-led teams rely on half-second increments of training, offensive buses that pull out onto the road before the defensive buses, reservations at the same hotel, exact routes to the stadium, and laminated cards that give players all the possible instructions a laminated card can provide. Losing power meant that precise routine had just been smacked by a meteor.

All the teams' mechanical-electrical needs were inaccessible. There was no last-minute film study, the team's brunch was cold pizza, and there was no team meeting because there was no light.

When Tony and his defensive mates took the field, they were feeling discombobulated—just as the offense was.

Despite being in the zone just two games ago, Tony's efforts could not help prevent an early game pasting by an unranked

Fighting Illini squad. The weather offered no solace for the embattled Lions. It was a foggy day in Champaign-Urbana; a good metaphor for what the Lions were battling through.

"This is an amazing game," Tony mused on the field as his team went down 21–0 in the first quarter. Illinois sophomore phenom Simeon Rice was having his way from his defensive end position, blasting past the Lions players as if he were cutting in line at a daycare lunchroom.

Collins was having no luck throwing because he had no time to unload the football. The Lions were losing to a team that hadn't remotely demonstrated this kind of firepower all season. Tony could afford to be clinical in the heat of battle. Just as his father had faced a veteran North Carolina State team a generation previous, these Lions were battle-tested and not prone to panic.

By the second quarter, both offense and defense had calmed down and gone to work. The defense stopped the point hemorrhaging while the offense narrowed the score. The Lions trailed by 10 points midway through the fourth quarter.

Junior fullback Brian Milne was in full song against Illinois. He had scored two touchdowns from within six yards. But for the Lions to win the game, the team would have to travel 96 yards in the final 6:07 of the game. They trailed 31–28.

Sweaty, tired, and helmetless, Tony watched from the sidelines. He held hands with his teammates. Collectively, they were trying to will the ball into the end zone.

Collins and his receivers chose that series of plays to stand tall. Despite the thick fog on the field, Collins completed a scorching 13 of 15 passes in the fourth quarter and was seven-for-seven on the final drive.

In the closing seconds of the game, with the ball two yards from the goal, Milne powered in his third touchdown for a come-from-behind 35–31 win over Illinois. It was the biggest deficit—21 points—a Paterno team had ever overcome.

Down to Business	The lessons the Pittmans took away from this series of football games are myriad. Most important, each learned that the job must be done by a team effort. Neither require the lesson of spelling out the word team and noting the lack of an I, because those minutes spent on the sidelines as young men remain indelible in their minds. They've lived the Blue Line, eaten and breathed teamwork, so there's no need for vocabulary parlor tricks.

Belong to a Team You Trust

Charlie's tense moments against North Carolina State were echoed in Tony's experience against Illinois three decades later. Time and circumstance might have been slightly different, but each learned that they had to rely on the talents and judgment of their teammates and coaches. Charlie crossed his fingers for a defensive stop, while Tony prayed for an offensive play.

For athletes and nonathletes alike, the Pittmans garnered a bit of wisdom beyond the Blue Line that has served them well in both sports and business.

The lesson is: relying on teamwork means manipulating the odds in your favor. If you're a multimillion-dollar lottery winner or Bill Gates, you can ignore this advice. But if you're not, you do so at your own peril.

Play the Odds

Jocks play the odds. Being part of a team means you are playing the odds in your favor in regard to a specific goal. Period. The team has to come first or your odds of success take a walk down to the root cellar.

Joe Paterno greatly admired Charlie's overall athletic ability, but he would not suddenly have Charlie Pittman kick a field goal because he wouldn't know what to expect in that situation. That would be high-risk gambling.

Prior to the North Carolina State game in 1967, the Penn State defense had been examined for its goal line stand ability in countless practice situations. Paterno knew who the weak links were and replaced them. He had a reckoning of who was conditioned enough to excel in the fourth quarter versus those who fizzled out.

Against Illinois in 1994, he knew it was very unlikely his offense would be shut out and thus the Lions needed simply to let the storm wear itself out and work to remain close enough for a final score. He played the odds.

But American business is filled with high-rolling gamblers who never met a long shot they didn't like. Too often, an all-for-one attitude flies in the face of standard business practices. After all, this is the nation where Enron, Tyco, MCI, and Drexel Burnham Lambert grew to gargantuan proportions with high-rolling individuals at the helm.

Being reminded that no loyalty is owed to either employer or employee is almost as common nowadays as saying hello.

"It's hard to see a team concept in the business world," Tony says. "In my first year of business, I was a little surprised at how, for some, much of everyday business was trying to keep a low profile and not draw any notice."

Define Your Objectives—Clearly

In the business world, with its goals that may not be clear-cut and objectives that may be fluid, it is vital that the player—you— define your objectives as specifically as possible. In earlier chapters we talked about setting your season and your goals. The reason for that is clarity. If a promotion is your goal, are you satisfied if you receive a lateral promotion? Probably not.

Be specific.

And when you are specific about what you do, you can be a better teammate and the odds begin to favor you. On the football field, players play specific positions despite most having the ability to play more than one position.

Find Your Creativity within the Team Framework

Being part of a team, letting go of the "me first" paradigm, is a paradox. You can find your creativity within the confines of your position if you try. Tony was not permitted to run the ball in a game unless he intercepted it; Charlie could not tackle in a game unless a play was broken and the opponents' defense recovered the ball. But within their roles of running back and cornerback each could explore the role in-depth and shine to his heart's content.

In an America ruled by the cult of personality, generalists often get our attention. Writer-director-producer Steven Spielberg has made a billion dollars using disparate talents. Oprah Winfrey has made a billion dollars with her television show, magazine, books, and sundry other products.

But each has a niche talent that he or she supports with quality teams. Spielberg directs. Oprah chats. When Oprah's producer doesn't do the job, she is replaced. If Spielberg's director of photography loses his touch, he is gone. The team continues.

The same goes for a football team. But what is a clear message on the gridiron has grown less so in the business world, as Tony noted.

A quick question: why are football teams and military operations so similar? After all, there are the uniforms, the need to acquire real estate forcefully, and strategies meant to exploit opponents' weaknesses. Taking the analogy further, there are football camps that feel like boot camp and "drills" meant to hone skills in both disciplines.

Part of the answer is to allow a player or recruit to feel part of something greater by minimizing the effect of individuality. Don't go up in arms. This isn't necessarily a value judgment on individuality so much as it is a "time and place" argument. Individuality is highly prized in the art world and in a number of solo pursuits, but it has a time and place on both the football and military fields.

Grand Goals Are Usually Collective Goals

The primary reason that the military and football bear such similarities to one another is because neither endeavor can be executed solely by individuals. Their goals, "for God, country, and freedom" or "for a national championship," are too massive. For such large goals there will always be pushback—other nations have committed armies, other football teams have huge, strong guys. So, too, the cooperative strategy must be massive.

Practice So Much That the Real Thing Seems Easy

Former Penn State defensive standout Andre Collins, who does the best impersonation of Joe Paterno known to humankind and now works as the director of retired players in the NFL Players' Association, fondly recalls Paterno's attention to detail. Collins had a long, successful career in the NFL for the Washington Redskins, Cincinnati Bengals, Chicago Bears, and Detroit Lions, for which he says he was well prepared. He credits Paterno's practices, which he describes as one long massive overload of preparation.

"The odds were that there'd be nothing in a game that would faze us," Collins says. "Joe's practices were so hard that the games seemed easy."

Even in such a regimented system, individuality will always try to make itself known. Charles Pittman believes wholeheartedly in the Penn State way. He respects the plain blue and white uniforms and would be one of the first to complain if Penn State went the way of every other university and allowed players' names to be sewn on the backs of their uniforms. But Charlie Pittman wore spats when he played. It was his individual statement.

The individual will tend to say, "Look at me. I can do this." Or, "I want to do this my way." Football and the military both have one reply to both statements: "Show me if you can."

Privates become generals by proving their mettle—within the system. Benchwarmers become starters by proving their talent—within the system.

An Ode to Creativity

Teamwork doesn't try to stamp out creativity—far from it. It seeks to engage it within the confines of the field of competition, be it sports or business. Teamwork lets the players show themselves as they truly are, not how they wish they could be.

Football is a team sport that relies heavily on testing parameters and playing the odds. Creativity in football is a single, beautiful black rose on a carefully tended, exactly measured plot of garden. It is Charlie Pittman's decision to cut back to midfield with an impossibly long stride that starts with a pirouette in front of a grunting, 300-pound lineman and culminates in a leaping touchdown 40 yards downfield.

Creativity is a Tony Pittman hurdle over a falling opponent, sensing a half-step change of direction by his man, making a matching change backward at full speed and springing into the air just as the football starts to descend and knocking it to the ground.

If creativity is considered a spur-of-the-moment leap off the high dive, teamwork may best be described as a series of collaborative test jumps off of increasingly higher diving boards. Either way, the jump is made.

For Charles, playing the odds is framed best by constructing a strong team. One of his most cherished lessons taken from football is that it is never about knocking people down; rather, it is about picking them up. He manages his business teams based on the Penn State principles of employees earning responsibility and being given the opportunity to show their capabilities.

South Bend Tribune managing editor Tim Harmon is a subordinate of Charles Pittman's, and he sees Charlie's dedication to his team on a daily basis.

"Charles is concerned about goals and motivation," Harmon says. "He is very clear about goals and very strong in motivation. I think one of the things he learned from sports is you motivate different people different ways. Sometimes you motivate the same people different ways. If you fall short, he can make you feel really bad about that.

"It takes a while to understand that approach. Basically, he says, 'Let me know what you need to be successful and I then I expect you to be successful.' He puts his money where his mouth is. He has astounded me at the speed at which he has done that."

Harmon recalls a situation where Charles went the extra yard for his "team."

"I've seen some interesting flashes of how he gets things done," Harmon says. "We'd interviewed a young woman at Michigan in a job fair. We asked her to come to South Bend, but she didn't have enough experience for a paper of our size. She said she'd like to come to Schurz [the parent company]. I was talking with the editor of our Noblesville paper. I asked if he could give her an internship to keep her interested in us. They didn't have it available. A position was in our budget and I was allowed to fill it. But when I hung up, it was Friday at 7:00 PM. She needed an answer. I knew if I could forgive that position at our paper for the summer and tell their editor to hire her as an intern, we'd keep her in our camp. But I also knew I couldn't do it without executive approval.

"I called Charles at home. He was out in his yard cutting his grass. At 9:00 PM on Friday night he wrote an e-mail approving it. If he'd waited until Monday, we would have lost her. She did the internship, she was hired full time by Noblesville, she worked there for a year and then came here. Right now, she's one of our stars. Those are the little things he does."

Now that you can recite "the team comes first" and "a team plays the odds" in your sleep, the underlying need is to establish a belief in the system you choose or create.

Penn State is a system like any other. It is imperfect because no single system works perfectly for all people. Its bedrock tenets of trust, loyalty, earned responsibility, collective achievement, and established hierarchy don't work for everyone. These concepts sound like no-brainer positives, but concepts are abstractions.

Penn State achieves those concepts with concrete rules that start to become problematic for some young people: no wearing hats indoors, facial hair restrictions, curfews, suits worn on game travel days, no tardiness—those are the rules. Which one of those rules is a synonym for trust?

Sometimes the system doesn't seem to work at all. By 2004, for instance, the call for Paterno to step down had grown into a din. Between 2000 and 2004, Paterno had presided over a rare occurrence for modern Penn State football: the program lost 33 out of 59 games. His system seemed quaint compared to Miami, USC, Texas, and other "modern" programs.

Kids born in the late 1980s had video game attention spans and first-person shooter mentalities that the erudite Paterno could never relate to. After all, this was the same guy who made his only Heisman Trophy winner, John Cappelletti, toil as a defensive back before permitting him to return to the tailback position that he had starred in as a high schooler. How well would that work with a big, fast, and heavily recruited high school star circa 2007?

In Case You Weren't Paying Attention Before—You Have to Believe

Undefeated teams and undefeated people believe in the systems they choose for business success, and they've got to believe even harder when it doesn't work. Because if a system never fails, then it's not a system; it's a miracle machine.

"We believed in the system," Tony says. "Still, everyone within Joe's structure found their own way for going into a game. He just didn't like a lot of fooling around. Guys who figure out how to deal with it do well. They believe they can get past the nervousness and do the job. That's embodied, outside of football, by guys like [pro golfer] Tiger Woods. As good as he is, the thing he's best at is concentration, being in the moment.

"At Penn State, we could look at Joe's laminated cards and go through the steps and try to stay focused. I think the cards really helped with nervous energy. If it's a game day, this is what you do. It's all written down. In the most tense, pressure-packed moments, Joe had a way of reminding people that they were prepared. Success means trying not to get too uptight when a job needs to be done. Winners always visualize things going well for them."

Sports Logic—Pay Close Attention

In the business world, the lessons are undiluted—be a team player, play the odds, and believe in your system. And remember the lessons taught to Penn State's players by North Carolina State, Indiana, and Illinois. A win is what can happen at the end of a contest, but even if you don't lose, it doesn't mean you've won.

"The day before we played against Oregon in the Rose Bowl, my teammates and I watched Nebraska play Miami and win. That dashed our hopes for a national championship," Tony recalls. "So there's a knock on the door, somebody said Joe was calling us together because he wanted us to know that we still had to be ready to go out and play. 'I might be able to get some of these [number one] votes pointed to us,' Joe told us. And because it was Joe Paterno, that was just enough to make you go to sleep and say to yourself, 'We need to go out and get it done.' We didn't go out there and tank. We went out, and Ki-Jana Carter scored on the first play."

Certainly, the consensus championship still went to Nebraska, but just as in business, global forces aren't always fair.

But now that you are a smart, odds-figuring team player with a specific goal and a system you believe in, we're going to find some help for your career. Just keep reading.

> **WINNING IN LIFE**
> "My belief is that most business projects will definitely fail unless someone is appointed the leader. Someone has to own the project. Recognized ownership is nine-tenths of the game. You have to have an owner; that way there's only one throat to choke. And if you

choose to be that leader, you really have to believe the project is a good one and commit to having the project reach a successful end. Remember, these two outcomes aren't coincidental—failing project and no ownership. After you take the lead, then you've got to identify the major stakeholder and determine where the power lies: Who would care about it? Whose bonus or promotion is on the line if this doesn't happen? Go to them. Make a statement that says there must be ownership. This statement can't be a back door, in-the-closet agreement. Don't leave the room until everyone agrees on the principle and the person. Lack of ownership or fragmented ownership is a recipe for poor performance."

—*Tony Pittman*

CHAPTER 7

Looking for Paterno

Joe Paterno is a creature of habit, but oh, what habits! In one of the most remarkably consistent routines in college sports, he has led a group of a hundred of the nation's best young football players down a Beaver Stadium tunnel for more than 40 years. And whether it is Charlie Pittman's team, Tony Pittman's team, or his current one, the ritual reaches across time.

First, a pair or trio of Penn State's captains walk out onto the field with the referees for the coin toss.

A few yards behind, fresh from the team prayer, Paterno follows with the Nittany Lions trailing in his wake. He jams his hands into his khaki trousers and saunters under the awning with the azure and cream lion's head logo, a signature right-legged hitch in his gait. He checks his right wrist for the time and then…waits. Behind him—a head taller and so energized it looks like blue and white popcorn, jumping, fidgeting, ready to burst—is his team.

He always waits a few seconds, holds still for a zephyr across his broad cheeks that only he recognizes, whispering the time is right. He lifts his hand without turning around, points to the field and begins to trot out while the crowd explodes.

This is the essence and the curse of Joe Paterno. He is a rock star with a factory worker's sensibilities. Mick Jagger would love to have the audience he routinely draws. In a world where most people hold a job for five years and move on, he has punched the clock at Penn State since 1950. On average, six Division 1A football coaches have come and gone at other institutions in the time that Paterno has spent at Penn State.

While some people struggle to break routines, ruts, and sundry habitual behavior, Paterno embraces familiar moments such as his team's stadium entrance. And he is placed neatly in a box for his consistency: the old football coach.

Almost a lawyer, almost an NFL coach, he is Penn State football and has been since 1966. But don't mistake steadiness for unimaginativeness, nor should you take the factory worker analogy too far. Paterno didn't get to the top of the football world without the ego, smarts, and vision of a CEO.

For instance, the man is a tireless booster for Penn State and, along with Sue Paterno, he is a major benefactor of the school as well. The Paternos have donated more than $4 million to expand the Pattee Library at University Park, which is Penn State's main campus, and have helped to raise another $13.5 million in private donations for its construction. The expanded wing was named the Paterno Library in their honor.

Paterno is that entity that writers break into a cold sweat trying to describe with some accuracy—a passionate human being.

Somewhere, buried in the dry research journals of a government-funded study with more money than common sense, there are numbers that indicate left-handed people are statistically more likely to be geniuses or maniacs than the world's more numerous right-handers. Paterno is left-handed and, for both friends and foes, he seems to be a little maniacal and brilliant in equal measure.

At the close of the 2002 season, Paterno courted controversy with his decision to play defensive back Anwar Phillips in the Capital One Bowl game, a loss to Auburn. Phillips had been charged with sexual assault and was expelled from the university weeks before the game. Penn State president Graham Spanier openly criticized Paterno for the decision to allow an expelled student to play in the bowl game; it was a rare public spat that wasn't helped by the next season's 3–9 record, the worst in the Paterno Era.

The turn of the century hit Paterno's program hard. Discipline problems—never a real concern at the institution that engendered the Grand Experiment—began to pile up along with the losses. Paterno's reputation for being a gruff taskmaster who was prone to verbal criticisms had mutated. He seemed to have lost the fine point from his masterful motivational skills. Players on the team spoke of Paterno's constant harangues about responsibility and his making a show of dumping equipment from the lockers of players who been suspended in front of teammates.

Sports reporters in central Pennsylvania cast their eyebrows skyward on February 17, 2004, when Penn State's sports information department released a media announcement stating that offensive coordinator Fran Gantner was being promoted to associate director for football operations. Gantner was a sympathetic figure for the media; he had lost his wife, Karen, to a sudden brain aneurism in 2002 and had become a single father to his three sons. Sinister motives were ascribed to Gantner's departure from the sidelines. Though it was an upward move, it surprised many sportswriters who were certain he would follow Paterno as the Lions' head coach. Instead, an old Penn Stater, Galen Hall, former head coach for the University of Florida, was hired into the offensive coordinator spot. There must have been some kind of fallout, some opined. Others suggested that Gantner, one of the architects of Penn State's 1994 scoring machine and a good friend of Paterno's, was being bumped for Jay Paterno, the coach's son.

Nepotism. Ridicule of players. Flaunting the law. A groundswell of public criticism began and the rallying cry was Paterno's age: *He's too old. He's out of touch. The game has left him behind.*

What can one do when four decades of success seems to have evaporated? For Paterno, it meant reinvesting in the system, not abandoning it. But there were even cracks in Paterno's mighty ship of former football athletes. Smart, successful, driven, dedicated Nittany Lions were suggesting the admiral should retire.

Matt Millen was symptomatic of Paterno's plight. Millen had been an All-American defender for Paterno. Millen is a powerful businessman; like the Pittmans, he is one of thousands of Penn State football success stories that light up the business world after leaving Paterno's program. He played 12 years in the NFL and was a member of three winning Super Bowl teams, the Oakland Raiders, Los Angeles Raiders, and San Francisco 49ers, as well as being voted to a Pro Bowl in 1988. In 2001 he was hired from the broadcast booth to become CEO and general manager of the Detroit Lions.

Millen was not the only former player who believed it was time for Paterno to name a successor in 2004, but he stung Paterno by saying it to his face.

Paterno's reply was terse: "It's none of your business, Matt."

In the world of big-time college football, there are no warm and fuzzy characters. There are good men and then there are men you'd want to keep an eye on in the event of a bar fight. Paterno is a crusty, conservative Republican who wouldn't know Justin Timberlake or Britney Spears unless they were being tackled on the Kentucky bluegrass of Beaver Stadium. Players who play for him understand that he is an acquired taste. He is blunt; he is a dictator that doles out the one thing players care most about—playing time.

Being a Division 1A coach is not the best place to pull together a therapy group to reaffirm one's right to exist. The position requires thick skin and cold decisions. Players who are hurt are benched. Players who don't fit the system are dropped. Assistant coaches with ambition to be more are given the straight dope. Paterno has seen it all and toughened his heart enough to make the hard choices.

Still, the years from 2000 to 2004 provided fresh daily wounds for Paterno, from an inner-circle member like Millen suggesting he plan for a successor to the weekly public lashings by students carrying signs that read JoePa Must Go.

Charles and Tony listened to the talk, read the blogs and newspapers, and decided the action to take was to remain loyal to their former coach. Tony often would express support of Paterno on his podcast.

Both believed Joe would go when it was time for him to go. In their minds, he had earned that perk of employment. The Pittmans spoke with their old coach several times a year; April's Blue and White intra-squad game was always a homecoming.

Tony, always considering the angle of any situation, worried about how an awkward few years could spoil his former coach's reputation. Even to discuss Paterno's departure was a touchy subject. But the media wouldn't let go of that bone.

"Look at Paterno even this year [in 2006, coming off of an 11–1 2005 season]," Tony says. "He's lost his patience with the media and at one point he stopped talking to the media. I think he is having a real tough time in today's media environment because of the kinds of stories they think they need to run. With our [1994] team, we were what the Penn State people wanted us to be; no real off-the-field trouble, we were winning our games. So I think the media was pretty fair in covering the program and keeping most of it football related. Were they being fair with some of the recent teams? Probably not.

"I was interviewed by Ron Bracken of the *Centre Daily Times,* a writer who I respect, and has covered the program for years. Still, he quoted me in an article as saying, that '[Penn State] was killing me...' and that 'Saturdays used to be easy' when I was a player. Well, I had to call Penn State coaches and tell them that's not what I said. My point had been that it was tough to watch Penn State teams struggle. Of course, it was a tough time for everyone. Also, I had mentioned how Joe always worked us so hard in practice, especially on Tuesdays, that games would often seem easy to us. Well, put those two points together in the wrong fashion, and you can see how it gets messy very quickly."

Charles, in particular, had always been comfortable with speaking his mind with Paterno. He held an exalted position in Paterno's pantheon, forever esteemed as one of the Super Sophomores. Even more, in his playing days, Pittman was a field general with a calm demeanor, who helped keep the rambunctious dispositions of his fellow running backs in check on the field and off. If he had felt as Millen did, he would have come out and told Paterno.

"Joe and I have always been able to talk," Charles Pittman says. "About anything. There's been controversy before. As he was turning Penn State into a rising power in college football, the NCAA was considering raising the test scores that high school athletes needed to achieve to be eligible for scholarships. Joe had a lot of clout and he was in favor of raising the minimum score and I took a position against it. I felt it was a ploy to control the number of African Americans playing college sports.

"I told Joe that if you see someone trapped in a mine, or a ghetto, you don't help them by blocking the escape routes. What's needed are more escape routes.

"Joe turned to me and said, 'Charlie, if you only expect people to rise to a certain level that's what they will shoot for—and they will reach it.' He believed lowering standards would work against that striving. So, we had to agree to disagree."

Paterno has always respected Charles Pittman's advice, but these current difficulties were more personal. The support of Charles, Tony, and hundreds of other former players was flattering, but ultimately he had to resolve his situation by himself.

And it wasn't just the losing, even though he had experienced the first pair of consecutive losing records in his career. No, in Paterno's mind, his system was failing. It needed to be fixed, which meant he needed to do what he loved best: strategize and plan.

A wounded animal seeks out a safe place to lick its wounds and gain respite from the predators of the wild. Paterno's usual place for personal rebuilding is Penn State's state-of-the art football complex.

The Louis E. Lasch Football Building is a $15 million complex that contains Paterno's spacious office, a 150-seat high-tech auditorium, athletes' study area, and a 10,000-square-foot training facility with two-story windows. But Paterno didn't feel safe there anymore. Neither could he escape this new turn of events on the old Holuba Hall practice fields, much less Beaver Stadium. Before he could emerge triumphant, he needed to retreat to his inner sanctum.

Paterno's home is the modest, four-bedroom ranch-style home with a two-car garage he shares with his wife, Sue, on McKee Street. Poetically, for a man nearer the end of his career than the beginning, it is a left turn off of Sunset Park.

Paterno married Suzanne Pohland in 1962, and they raised five children, all of whom are Penn State graduates, in that house. The couple has two daughters, Diana Giegerich and Mary Kathryn Hort, and three sons, David, George Scott, and Joseph Jr., whom everyone calls Jay.

Paterno could catch his breath on McKee Street. Behind the tan and blush masonry of the 1960s-style structure and under the verdant canopy provided by the tangle of trees in his yard, Paterno could think.

Paterno retired to his den, with its high eastward-facing windows. On hundreds of Saturday mornings, he would rise at 4:00 AM to tweak the day's game plan and assess his team's capabilities in that room. His trophy shelf rests just below the windows, and it holds a half-century's worth of trophies and—devout Catholic that he is—a silver crucifix.

It might take the course of an afternoon, or a month of afternoons, spent considering all the variables, but Paterno would make the adjustment. Paterno is, after all, essentially a CEO who doesn't flinch when asking for multi-million-dollar donations from wealthy philanthropists. He understands the fickle nature of youth and yet has built an enduring legacy on a foundation created from the whims of young athletes.

For him, pressure is a fact of life, not an obstacle.

And he is the wellspring for a great many inspirational quotes that have inspired millions of people over the years. His own words were a good place to start as he searched for reinvigoration.

"Losing is heartbreaking. Losing your sense of excellence or worth is a tragedy," Paterno has said to players.

"You have to perform at a consistently higher level than others, that's the mark of a true professional," is another Paternoism.

Or there's this bit of prophecy, spoken by Paterno for a September 1969 *Sports Illustrated* interview. Paterno was being courted for the Pittsburgh Steelers' head coaching position and being offered enormous sums of money to join the professional ranks.

"Someday, when we're 3–7, I'll remind people how glad they said they were when I decided to stay," he said then.

That is the public Paterno—a quote machine that onlookers place on a pedestal. The private Paterno occasionally has his toes stepped on by the public JoePa.

"Joe once told us that he tried to order a pizza when he was hungry and Sue wasn't there to make him any dinner," recalls Tony. "This happened while I was there; he said the local delivery guys laughed at him when he gave his name as Joe Paterno ordering a pizza for delivery. They said, 'Yeah, right,' and hung up on him. So he couldn't get a pizza delivered."

Pizza delivery weaknesses notwithstanding, Paterno is much too savvy a man to give away the secrets or the timetable for his football problem solving, but the nature of his work means that any course changes are in the public domain almost as soon as he implements them.

If his first Grand Experiment meant recruiting scholars who happened to be athletes, to compete at the highest levels, then this sequel to the experiment would mean finding young men who could relate to old-fashioned ideals of trust, loyalty, and responsibility. It would be Paterno's Oil—the salve to fix an ailing program.

The world saw the changes Paterno made and, as expected, they were course corrections, not changes in destination.

The first change he made after the 2004 season was to be more active in all phases of the game. He would tweak recruiting staff duties and even spend time himself on the recruiting trail. Tony noted that he personally wrote letters and notes to high-level recruits such as Derrick Williams, a quarterback from Maryland, who was viewed as one of the best all-around athletes in the nation.

Secondly, he would spread the good word. Penn State wanted quality athletes and wouldn't tolerate some of the nonsense of recent years from its recruits.

Thirdly, he pulled a Babe Ruth and called one out of the park. Paterno was confident his 2005 season would be a turnaround from the disasters of 2003 and 2004. He needed a forum to tell naysayers: "Hold onto your pitchforks and torches. If we lose again, the monster surrenders."

On May 12, 2005, in front of an audience at the Duquesne Club in Pittsburgh, Paterno put his job on the line for the upcoming season.

"If we don't win some games, I've got to get my rear end out of here," Paterno said. "Simple as that."

The fourth step of Paterno's Grand Experiment, Phase II, was to win football games.

Simple.

Paterno's 2005 squad, led by versatile quarterback Michael Robinson, went 11–1 and quieted the restless mobs. Paterno couldn't have written a more satisfying comeback season if he had magically transported his den into the shadow of the Hollywood sign and written it himself.

Robinson, the season's hero, was a vintage Penn State product. The quarterback, who stands 6'1", weighs 226 pounds, and has a blazing 4.55-second speed in the 40-yard dash, was recruited by Penn State out of Varina High in his native Richmond, Virginia. Robinson started all four years there as quarterback. But Paterno shifted him from position to position as an underclassman. Robinson played running back, slotback, tailback, split end, and returned punts—wherever the coach thought to put him. He earned scholastic All-American honors for three straight years. And, despite winning only seven of 23 games in his sophomore and junior years, Robinson remained the good soldier. The pathos in his story included temporary paralysis after being tackled by Wisconsin defensive end Erasmus James. Robinson was taken to a hospital after being knocked unconscious. He had no feeling on the left side of his body for nearly an hour.

The biggest blemish on Robinson's reputation was a 4:00 AM incident on February 7, 2003, during the Alpha Phi Alpha Black Ice skate party at the school's Greenburg Ice Pavilion. A fight broke out and Robinson and two of his teammates were involved. Robinson was pushed into a glass trophy case and sustained a serious cut behind his left ear. After an investigation into the brawl, Paterno suspended Matthew Rice and Ed Johnson from summer practice. He determined that Robinson's involvement never went beyond defending himself, so he placed him on probationary status.

With a winning record, the lapsed faithful returned. Robinson played the leading man, and Paterno's 2005 Nittany Lions uncorked a 10–1 regular season record, losing only a hotly contested 27–25 shocker to Michigan. Michigan won the game with a 10-yard touchdown pass from Chad Henne to Mario Manningham on the final play and final second of the game. That second might not have been available if Michigan head coach Lloyd Carr had not asked for and received an additional two seconds back onto the clock. Carr told officials that the timekeeper had made an error and they agreed.

At 7–1 in the Big Ten, Paterno was forever young in the eyes of fans. All was forgiven. After all, there was a bowl game to consider.

Once again, the performance of the Nittany Lions would put Hollywood to shame.

On January 3, 2006, Paterno and his number-three ranked Nittany Lions defeated the 22nd-ranked Florida State Seminoles, 26–23 in three overtimes in the FedEx Orange Bowl. It was the third time the teams had met in a bowl game—and the first without a Pittman starting.

Besides the obvious drama of an old-fashioned barnburner of a game, Paterno was facing his old friend, Bobby Bowden. The two men on the sidelines were the oldest active coaches in Division 1A.

In the early morning hours of January 4, 2006, the Lions were 11–1. Paterno might be a creature of habit, but he didn't set records for longevity and winning seasons by failing to adapt.

Paterno's Oil had worked. A few months later, on May 16, 2006, he and Bowden were elected to the College Football Hall of Fame.

Perhaps sensing that neither man would retire anytime soon, the National Football Foundation changed its rules for Hall of Fame entry. The new rules permitted any coach 75 or older to be eligible. Like a maitre d' to the best booths at Spago, the Hall of Fame waved Paterno and Bowden in with a low bow and a theatrical sweep of the arm.

The Duquesne speech seemed like it was made by another man, a lifetime away by the time spring of 2006 rolled around.

It was the Big Ten's media day and Paterno was in a mood to chuckle.

He told the story to the press that he had spent time with some of his 14 grandchildren after the end of the 2005 season and the extra activity was causing problems with his legs. He decided to see a doctor.

"I went to get a physical, I hadn't had a physical for nine or 10 years," Paterno said. "So, I took it and the doc said you can coach nine or 10 more years. I went back [to my coaching staff] and said, 'The doc said I can coach for nine or 10 more years.' You never saw so many guys put their heads down so fast!"

Down to Business	In 25 words or less, without using the phrase "football coach," describe Joe Paterno. Then, take another 25 words to describe your superior at your own organization—no profanity allowed. It's a rhetorical exercise, so put your pen down. What is important to remember is this: one of the words you use should be "complex."

Your Potential Champion Will Be a Complex Individual—Act Accordingly

Paterno is likely no more or less complex than any high-level corporate executive you will run into in your professional life. Engaging them can be difficult, often because of lack of access, but when you do engage an executive-level person, remember there is a human being there. In the business world, these movers and shakers can send careers skyward. Paterno, as noted above, was a champion for Michael Robinson even if his decision to continually switch his positions might have frustrated many players.

Joe Paterno is an icon—but his job isn't iconic. He's a football coach who has CEO-type powers. Because his product is each year's Nittany Lions football team, he has a different market than Charles Pittman does as senior vice-president of a media company. But his duties mirror Pittman's nicely:

Oversee creation of a consistent, quality product
Evolve corporate structure to support production
Manage public scrutiny
Negotiate downturns in supplies or markets
Track future market trends and opportunities
Make decisions for the greater good of the organization
Enhance shareholder value

Like Paterno, Charles, Tony, and you, there are hundreds of factors that may affect you on the job—family, personal distractions, or health or financial issues. If you are not experiencing those factors firsthand, it's easy to judge and easier still to misinterpret.

Looking toward the mountaintop, some decisions look heartless. Was Fran Ganter's bump upstairs cruelty, or a reward for a dedicated employee who would now have time for his sons who were coping without their mother?

Suspending players and tossing their gear on the floor in front of their teammates may be construed as mean-spirited...or motivational.

Allowing Anwar Phillips to play a bowl game after being accused of sexual assault might be self-serving, or it might mean Paterno was privy to facts in that sensitive matter he didn't care to share with the world at large.

If heavy is the head that wears the crown in your organization, lighten his or her load and in the process you'll advance your own career. While you're at it, always remember the complexity of the individual you select as a champion. That should cancel out any thoughts of brown-nosing, something Charles says is a big no-no. Intelligent people will see through it and it could derail your efforts.

A Champion Defined

In Charles's lexicon, a champion is someone who can make your job a little easier and who can help you navigate successfully up the organization.

The former running back describes champions as metaphoric offensive linemen who open the gap for you to bust through.

"A champion is someone who has the power in your organization and can make things happen. Most of the people in a company can say no. Find the ones who can say yes," Charles suggests. "You have to have enough to offer that they will invite you in. And you will have to play company politics. The guy who says, 'I'm not going to play politics,' is playing politics without knowing it. Plus, he's losing!"

Obviously, women and men at the top must make their own decisions because they are the ones who are responsible for corporate direction. But Charles recommends that anyone who wants to advance in his or her career have a champion.

Develop Relationships or Perish on the Vine

"I've said it many times and I always give young people this advice," Charles says. "In business, the importance of developing relationships is equally important to the level of skill or talent you possess. Managing or controlling business relationships is an incredibly important skill. People enjoy doing business with people they like and respect. You may not be best with the Xs and Os, but if you are able to cultivate relationships, you are more likely to move forward."

Ted Junker of Marine Bank, Ed Mead of Times Publishing Company, Jim Schurz of Schurz Communications, Inc., Rolfe Neill of the *Charlotte Observer*, and Ron Rickman and Dick Gottlieb of Lee Enterprises have all been champions for Pittman.

"These men are captains of industry," Charles says. "They don't have time to waste, so I've always found it beneficial to truth-tell to the people who have power. Most times, they appreciate it, and if they don't, you have to consider you're in the wrong organization."

Charles says people will notice you after you've selected a champion and that has to be expected. And they begin associating you with your champion.

"When I started with Times Publishing, I was this new guy walking into a big meeting with [chair of the company] Ed Mead and people would notice that he asked me questions, solicited my opinion," he recalls. "In Charlotte, [publisher] Rolfe Neill would walk with me down the halls, or he'd stop by my office. Or in my position at Marine Bank, when I was seen talking with Ted Junker, the president of bank—those situations gave me a perceived power that I really didn't have."

Four Rules for Finding a Champion

FIRST RULE: YOU ONLY GET ONE TRY

There are several rules involved in finding a champion. The most important rule is to make one and only one selection. You don't want your champion to be a second choice—news gets around. Your first choice should be your only choice. Lots of pressure, right? Welcome to the world of business.

The pressure of making the right choice should help you see more clearly how power is distributed in your company. Look closely to see who has it, and gauge the likelihood of it being shared with you.

SECOND RULE: EXPECT MOVEMENT WITHIN 90 DAYS

Another rule is to make sure your champion does something positive for your career in 90 days or less. Results matter. If you choose the president of your company and don't see her for the next year, it was a bad choice. And this is a Pittman–Paterno–Penn State strategy, which means you have to be aware of time, so mark your calendars. If your champion agrees to mentor you on January 1, by April 1 you should see results.

THIRD RULE: SAY THE WORDS!

Ask directly for mentoring from your champion. Say the words, "Will you be my champion?" and then listen carefully. Also, ensure that this person is signing up for what you need them to do. One of humanity's shortcomings is hearing what one wants to hear. Is that yes actually a no? Know the difference. Choose not to be an accomplice to a passive no. And, conversely, be thankful for a direct, honest no. It saves you time, it lets you know where you stand, and those bits of knowledge are great accomplishments in and of themselves.

FOURTH RULE: VIOLATE YOUR PRINCIPLES

"I know that some people will see the whole process as selling out, a violation of their principles and values," Pittman says. "They believe only performance merits placement and position. But if they think of that as a principle, then it's a principle that needs to be violated.

"That kind of thinking assumes that performance exists in a vacuum—it doesn't. In the business world, my performance affects the performance of others. That creates organizational politics. And it's in your best interest to understand those politics and understand power."

Charles and Tony Pittman pride themselves on being diligent observers—a skill that helped on the football field and in boardrooms. Cultivate your own powers of observation. Who has the real power—the power of yes in your organization?

A Champion in Action

Charles played two years of professional football in the NFL, with the St. Louis Cardinals in 1970 and the Baltimore Colts in 1971. His class of 1970 contemporaries had a two-year head start on him when he entered the business world.

In 1972, Paterno became the champion that started Charles's business career. After talking him into leaving an unsatisfying NFL stint, Paterno recommended Charles for a job with Junker's Marine Bank. Junker was a member of the Penn State family and took him on.

Things You Owe Your Champion

Charles says showing commitment to your organization is essential; as is having a good work ethic and continually striving for positive change in the company.

"It's not just about getting information from your champion," he says. "You have to let him know you're into your career. You need to share with him, advise him, and let him know you're serious.

"You also have to be respectful of people's time," he added. "It's your job as the subordinate to be on top of that. Don't be overbearing or wear out your welcome. That threshold is different from person to person, but you should find out what's appropriate based on the type of relationship you have.

"If you're working day to day with your champion, seeing him once or twice a week is okay. If you don't work with him, it might be once every two to three months. Don't make the mistake of calling only when you need something. Ask about him. Have friendly conversations. Give updates on your career. Find out what he's doing."

Charles says people in power need to have subordinates tell the truth to them, which makes sense since most people like to make decisions based on factual information. He suggests offering your opinion when appropriate.

"Your champion might want to bounce something off of someone," Charles says. "That shows he values your opinion, and often people in charge are appreciative."

Think Like a Woman

Charles says the examples of his mother and his older sister Rosalind have always helped him in his efforts to find a champion and, more important, in being a champion himself. His mother and sister were strong women who affected his perceptions of the traditional male-female dynamic. He has an abiding respect for the perspective of women.

"I don't like it when I attend a meeting and there are no women there," he says. "One of my secrets is I want to think like a woman [in many situations]. Sure, men are recognized for their aggressiveness and competitive natures, but women are more direct. They are truth-tellers and don't BS you as much. They're not swayed by appearances. Too often, in my experience, men look for ways not to do things."

A Champion Speaks Up

Edward Mead, chair of the Times Publishing Company based in Erie, Pennsylvania, recalls that Charles was a good fit for his corporation. Mead hired him after he left Marine Bank, also in Erie.

"We were looking for a promotion manager and I knew him pretty well," Mead says. "Among other things, Charles is a great people person. He had become well-known in Erie as a guy who liked people. I also appreciated the fact that he was this ex-professional football player who wasn't carrying that on his sleeves. He knew he was good at business, but he worked with people without a trace of attitude. To this day, 15 years after he left, there are still women in the classified department who still talk fondly about him."

Charles's strengths may not be your own, but his talent for finding a champion, such as Ed Mead, can be.

Mead's family was a cofounder of what would eventually become the Times Publishing Company back in 1888. He and his family are powerful and well-connected in central Pennsylvania. Charles was coming from a job at a bank with no experience in the newspaper industry.

Mead took a chance on the 32-year-old family man.

Both men profited. As with Paterno, Charles had another champion, someone who believed in his talents

"I consider Charles a very good friend," Mead says. "We have a good relationship. I'm a great admirer of his because I've seen what he can do. He displays tremendous dedication to his kids, his mother. He's just one hell of a good guy. I know connections help, but if you don't produce—as Charles did—it's just another door. You've got to be able to do more than walk in a door."

WINNING IN LIFE

"I'll tell you this, in any fight it's the guy who's willing to die who's gonna win that inch. And I know, if I'm gonna have any life anymore it's because I'm still willing to fight and die for that inch, because that's what living is, the six inches in front of your face. Now, I can't make you do it. You've got to look at the guy next to you, look into his eyes. Now, I think you're going to see a guy who will go that inch with you. You're gonna see a guy who will sacrifice himself for this team, because he knows when it comes down to it you're gonna do the same for him. That's a team, gentlemen, and either we heal—now—as a team, or we will die as individuals. That's football guys, that's all it is. Now what are you gonna do?"

—Al Pacino in *Any Given Sunday*

PART III

Game Time

CHAPTER 8

If You Don't Know Where You're Going, Anyplace Will Do

Joe Paterno hates running up the score on overmatched opponents. Maybe it's the blood and sweat that he sees kids from his own program pour out on a weekly basis; maybe his perspective suggests football is a diversion, not a life-or-death matter, and should be fun. But he was finding it hard to hold the score down against the Navy Midshipmen on September 20, 1969. It was the third year together for his first recruiting class and they had jelled into a formidable machine. That machine was rolling downhill and the brakes were nowhere to be found. Lions linebackers Mike Reid and Steve Smear, in particular, were having their way with rookie coach Rick Forzano's running backs. They smashed them back behind the line of scrimmage or stopped them for no gain a dozen times before the first half ended. On the offense's side of the ball, Charlie was continuing his streak of superlative games. He had an amazing junior year in 1968; he gained 950 yards on 186 rushes and caught 14 passes for 196—more than 1,000 yards in all-purpose yards. Though slowed by ankle and knee injuries that kept him out of heavy contact practices, Pittman was starting 1969 with a bang.

"I remember that Navy game," former New York Giants general manager Ernie Accorsi recalls. Accorsi is a Hershey, Pennsylvania, native and has long been a huge Lions fan. In 1968 he worked for the Penn State football PR department. "It brought to mind the kinds of games Lenny Moore had back in 1955," he says. "Lenny was Penn State's first great back—one of the five greatest backs in the history of the game. Charlie was the next great back. Against Navy, Charlie scored a touchdown on a first down. It was one of the greatest seven- or eight-yard runs I'd ever seen. He broke about six tackles, and for the game he gained more than a hundred yards." Charlie gained 167 yards and scored two touchdowns en route to a 45–22 blowout of Navy. After the game, Baltimore Colts star running back Lenny Moore stopped by to meet him. "You had a great game, young man," Moore told him as he shook his hand. "I see you're bigger than me, but there's no sense in comparing things. You do your thing. I did mine." After the Navy game, members of the Penn State athletic department were considering pushing Charlie for the Heisman Trophy, college football's highest honor.

But the Lions' next game brought a change in Charlie's personal fortune.

1969—A Season of Champions
Colorado

Second-ranked Penn State was playing the Colorado Buffaloes at Beaver Stadium; it was Saturday, September 27, 1969, and Charlie had a bounty on his head.

Paterno tapped him to field the opening kickoff. Charlie had returned a kickoff 83 yards for a touchdown against West Virginia in 1967, and Paterno wanted to see if that lightning would strike twice.

"I remember receiving the kickoff and heading downfield and getting tackled," he says. "But I wasn't injured by the tackle. It happened in the pileup. Somebody just grabbed my right ankle and tried to twist it off! I never found out who did that."

For the remainder of the first quarter, Penn State, whose success had generated newfound respect for Eastern football, looked vulnerable. Trainers carried Charlie off and wrapped his ankle in ice, while Colorado's defense took advantage of the situation and pushed the Lions around the field.

How significant was Charlie's injury? Pennsylvania governor Raymond Shafer told the media he was "scared, especially after Pittman got hurt."

But sophomores Harris and Mitchell and senior fullback Abbey took up the offensive slack starting in the second quarter. Charlie's defensive mates made it a point to punish Colorado quarterback Bob Anderson, the nation's number one rushing quarterback. Anderson gained only four yards in 17 carries, threw just eight completions, and was intercepted three times.

The Lions scored 17 points in the second period and put the game away with a field goal and a 91-yard kickoff return by Paul Johnson. The final score was 27–3.

"That returned kick, in the Colorado game, somebody intentionally turned his ankle," says Accorsi. "It wasn't broken, but I'm sure calcium formed in it. It was pretty bad. He was never the same runner after that. That single play turned Charlie from a great back into a good back."

Paterno was worried. Charlie played a central role on the team. "We had good leadership," Paterno recalls. Charlie was one of the strongest leaders we ever had. He probably was the most underrated player we ever had. He could catch and run, and he always knew what was going on in the game. If I wanted to know how a game was really going, I'd grab him. He never got quite as much credit as the other guys."

The twisted ankle slowed him down considerably, and though he played against 20th-ranked Kansas State on the road, a new pair of Super Sophs was emerging—Mitchell and Harris. Both players would go on to fame in the NFL, but Harris would become a pop icon because of his Immaculate Reception with the Pittsburgh Steelers and as a starting back in four Super Bowl wins.

Kansas State

The Lions eked out their 22nd game without a loss, 17–14, and were glad to get it. Still, it was apparent that two stars were born:

Mitchell and Harris were nearly unstoppable against the Wildcats. If one didn't burn them, the other one did. Mitchell carried 19 times for 123 yards in the win.

Sportswriters, taking note of Pittman's injury and the close win against a serviceable Wildcats team, dropped Penn State's ranking from second in the nation to fifth.

West Virginia

West Virginia head coach Jim Carlen griped to the media about the slight to the team he called "Paterno's Boys."

"When the polls dropped Penn State from [the] number two spot, they might just as well have made us number one," he said forlornly.

Paterno made sure his players focused on the Mountaineers. The West Virginia program was better than it had been in years and was ranked 20th in the nation when they traveled to Happy Valley. The Mountaineers had the top-ranked rushing offense in the nation, their defense was ranked second in the nation, and they were undefeated. Still, it was all for naught.

Burkhart connected with Mitchell on the first touchdown drive for a streaking 67-yard pass that set the tone for the game. Two more scoring drives of 59 and 68 yards put 20 points on the scoreboard in a hurry.

West Virginia might have stood a chance if they had been able to get some offense going, but the Lions defense held them to 138 yards rushing.

After the game, Carlen joined a growing mob of Penn State believers, telling the media that he believed Penn State was better than number one ranked Ohio State.

Syracuse

Charlie and the rest of the Nittany Lions offense headed back onto the field for the start of the fourth quarter against the Syracuse Orangemen in their creaky old home field, Archbold Stadium.

Forty-two thousand Syracuse fans were screaming with happiness. October 18, 1969, had provided a wonderful Saturday afternoon for Orange football fans. Their unranked team was kicking the butts of the fifth-ranked team in the country.

Dennis Onkotz, running off the field, fairly spat at his offensive teammates: "When the hell are you guys going to do something?" Onkotz, a fiery biophysics major who was as brilliant in the classroom as he was brutal on the field, was tired and angry.

The Lions' defenders were doing what they could; George Landis had blocked two field goals, but the squad was frustrated by a very motivated Orange offense. Syracuse coach Ben Schwartzwalder felt Syracuse had been robbed of a victory by the Lions in 1968; he wanted blood, and his team was obliging. Running back Al Newton and quarterback Randy Zur scored for the Orange in the first half. Only a left-handed shoestring tackle by Neal Smith prevented Syracuse wingback Greg Allen from scoring on a fourth down sweep play. Instead of going up 21–0, the score remained 14–0.

"When we didn't score," Schwartzwalder said later, "I was sick."

Even without scoring on the play, Syracuse's defense was pushing the Lions' offense back onto its heels. It looked like a baseball game, three and out.

At halftime, Paterno led his troops into the locker room and made some adjustments. He was about to lead them back onto the field when he turned around as if he'd forgotten something.

The locker room was silent, waiting for Paterno to say what he needed to say—a reminder of the 23-game winning streak? A "win this one for the Gipper" exhortation?

"You guys are stinking up the place!" Paterno screamed. "You're playing lousy! I want you to go out there and, whatever you do, don't embarrass me! Don't embarrass this university, don't embarrass your parents, don't embarrass your team, and don't embarrass yourselves! Because the way you're playing, you're embarrassing everybody!"

Charlie had never seen Paterno so angry. Admittedly, they had played two crummy quarters of football, but it wasn't over.

"Don't embarrass my family?" Charlie mused. "Why would he say that?"

Generally, 21-year-old Charlie used the halftime rest period to review defenders' coverage or go over plays like 38 Sweep in his mind. He felt as if he'd been kicked in the stomach after Paterno's outburst. Pride and family were what he lived for. In a room full of a hundred guys, he felt like Joe had personally challenged him.

Winning was going to take some effort. Nothing had worked thus far offensively and extended time on the field had worn down the Lions' defense; they were dog tired by the fourth quarter. That was a credit to Syracuse's execution because, over a string of 14 games dating back to 1968, the high-powered Lions defense had garnered a national reputation by scoring as much as some offensive units—169 points courtesy of 40 pass interceptions, 22 fumble recoveries, two safeties, and five blocked punts. But time was ticking and several of the Lions' defenders were breathing heavily; there might not be any more rabbits to pull out of the hat.

Trotting to the huddle, Charlie shouted to his backfield mates.

"Fourth quarter's ours, you guys! We own it. Come on Lydell, Franco; we gotta do this!"

"I'm with you," Harris said.

"Let's find a way to do it," Mitchell answered.

The Lions ran out of that tunnel with Paterno's words ringing in their ears and immediately fell flat in the third quarter, as well.

"Oh, we were stinking up the place in the third quarter, too," Pittman recalls. "But as the quarter wore on, we started to do the little things right: a short gain here, a strong block there. The fourth quarter we knew would be ours."

Early in the fourth quarter, offensive coordinator George Welsh called for a draw play and Harris rumbled for a big gain. The yardage seemed to unclog the offense. Charlie's number was called for a long pass play down the left sideline. Burkhart nearly put it into Charlie's hands but before the football descended, Syracuse linebacker Richard Kokosky climbed onto his back.

Pass interference.

Schwartzwalder screamed bloody murder at that call. He ran onto the field, chasing down the officials as the crowd rained down boos. Penn State had the ball at the 4-yard line.

Mitchell bulled the ball in on the next play. Touchdown. Syracuse's lead was down to 14–6. Instead of going for a field goal, Paterno called for a two-point conversion. Burkhart was to hit Harris with a swing pass.

"I didn't know what Joe was thinking," Charlie said later. "But I knew he was smart enough to think ahead. He knew he wasn't going to play for a tie, so he was going to have to go for two on one of the drives. He figured our defense wasn't going to let them score any more points."

The play failed. But a flag was thrown. The field judge called holding on Syracuse's Don Dorr. The Lions had a reprieve. Paterno called 18 Sweep, a straight power sweep to the fullback. Harris ran in the score from the left to make it 14–8. Once again, Schwartzwalder was apoplectic.

With minutes left in the game and Syracuse unable to score—as Paterno had predicted—the Lions' defense showed it had a little magic left when Ham, a future Hall of Famer, deflected a Syracuse punt and the Lions caught it on the Orange 39-yard line.

Two plays later, Burkhart faked to Charlie off tackle on the play 56 Scissors and handed off to Harris. Harris split the defense and scrambled 36 yards for a touchdown to tie the game, 14–14.

Kicker Mike Reitz's extra point made the final 15–14. Penn State had won its 24th game in the streak.

"The thought of us losing never entered our minds that day," Charlie said later. "We knew we played lousy, but we hadn't fired our best shots yet. When you have a streak like that, you don't think, 'Oh, the streak's going to end.' You think, 'We're going to find a way to win this. When are we going to make the play that pulls this out?'"

Just getting to this point was indicative of Charlie's character, not to mention his threshold for pain. He'd been nicked and dinged many times in his career, but the severity of his ankle injury had forced him to adapt his running style—the style he had spent his entire childhood developing. He was a long-strider who needed the full range of movement of his ankles to make the gravity-bending moves that duped defenders.

Had his running style been based on power and contact, the injury wouldn't have required as much adjustment. Not being physically able to run as he once had was difficult to accept. Still, he pushed through the pain. By season's end he would do something that would stand out generations later—in a backfield full of future All-Americans, he was the leading rusher.

By October 25, when they played Ohio at home, the Lions, for a second time that season, had won a game and dropped in the polls. This time they fell to number eight. Paterno assured the media that he didn't care to comment on what the pollsters were doing with his team's rankings at that time, but he warned they'd best have their act together by the end of the year.

"Twenty-four games without a loss and they've dropped us in the polls?" Paterno wondered aloud to his assistant coaches. Eastern football's reputation for being an inferior game was harder to shake than he thought. He was especially surprised by the drops because, while both Kansas State and Colorado had gone on to upset some teams from "real football country," his team had beaten both of those teams.

Ohio University

Charlie was adapting his game well and played a strong game against Ohio. As ever, the Penn State defense set up several scores with their frenzied scrambles around the field. They blocked two punts to set up two touchdowns for the offense, and safety Neal

Smith intercepted a pass and took it all the way for a touchdown. Mitchell and Harris ran wild over their overmatched opponents, and the Lions controlled the game from start to finish for a 42–3 win.

But the true shock and awe would be on display against their next opponent. It had taken five games, but Charlie was beginning to approximate his old running style.

Boston College

On November 1, Penn State put on a historic show when all three backs—Charlie, Harris, and Mitchell—ran for more than 100 yards apiece. For the first time in a long time, the offense led the charge. State's defense was caught off guard by the Eagles and allowed 13 points in the first half. The Lions were trailing as late as midway through the third quarter, when a sizzling ground game caught fire and began scoring points. Onkotz joined in on the offensive fun by returning a punt 48 yards for his first touchdown of the season.

After the Boston College win, 38–16, the media finally did the logical thing and rewarded Penn State for winning football games. The victory gave the Lions a bounce from number eight to number five.

Maryland

Charlie provided the offensive hammer for State by scoring three touchdowns. He scored the 24th, 25th, and 26th touchdowns of his career, overtaking Lenny Moore in that category. The Lions won 48–0, and Charlie gave Maryland's coach one last glimpse of the talent he possessed and the Terrapins missed out on.

As Penn State chalked up its 27th game without a loss, the real talk of the college football world was the Ohio State Buckeyes of the esteemed Big Ten conference. In 1969, Ohio State head coach Woody Hayes was the undisputed king of football. Some sportswriters went so far as to say that any claims teams like Penn State and Texas (ranked number three) had on the top spot were "frivolous." Hayes's team was a man among boys. His defense was considered to be the best in the nation—and so was his offense.

The only real competition either squad had was in practice against each other. Sure, humans landed on the moon, but no human teams would be beating these Buckeyes any time soon.

Closing Out the Season

Penn State closed out its amazing run with two strong showings: a 27–7 win against Pittsburgh and a 33–8 pasting of North Carolina State.

But the real game was being played off the field as the jockeying for bowl bids began.

"It is one of the grave injustices in the history of college football how that played out," recalls Accorsi. "We had a chance to go to the Cotton Bowl [an invitation Texas had already accepted], but Ohio State had two games to go. When they beat Purdue with [quarterback] Mike Phipps, Joe was thinking, 'Okay, that's it.' All they had to do was close out that last game and play for the national championship in the Rose Bowl. [At the time, the Rose Bowl only featured Big Ten and Pac 10 teams, and Penn State was an independent]. They were playing Michigan on the road and it was Bo's [head coach Bo Schembechler's] first year. The year before, they scored 50 points against Michigan when they beat them.

"So we elected to go to Miami. We remembered that Syracuse had had some difficulties regarding their black players in 1959 [in the Cotton Bowl]. We weren't thrilled with the prospect of dealing with that."

Surprise. Michigan beat Ohio State, which changed the college football universe as surely as the big bang had changed the real one. Texas was the new number one—and they were playing in the Cotton Bowl.

"Texas would not have beaten that [Penn State] team," Accorsi insists. "It would not have been close. They might have scored—maybe once. But that backfield! Pittman, Mitchell, and Harris. They would have had a field day. There was a bias against us; we were equated with Ivy League. But we beat Kansas with John

Riggins and Bobby Douglass. It's a tragedy that team didn't win a national championship. It's one of the great college football teams of all time."

That great team was stuck with a commitment to a bowl game that guaranteed they wouldn't be playing for a national championship. The only way for the Lions to become number one was if Texas lost to Notre Dame. The Fighting Irish were playing in their first bowl game in 45 years. Penn State's chances didn't look good.

But despite the rust of nearly half a century, Notre Dame almost pulled off the upset. Quarterback Joe Theismann would set a Cotton Bowl record by passing for 231 yards with 17 completions and two touchdowns

"We were standing in the lobby of the Balmoral Hotel in Miami, watching the Cotton Bowl," Accorsi remembers. "Theismann hits [Tom] Gatewood for a gain. We were cheering. It was emotional for us; and when Texas won [21–17] it took all the air from under our wings. I thought it was going to be bad for us [in our game against Missouri]."

Missouri: The Orange Bowl

Accorsi needn't have worried. At 28–0–1, these Lions were battle-tested, and distractions didn't weaken their collective focus. Riots at home, the screams of opposing coaches, extra players on the field, twisted ankles, injured knees—it didn't matter. This group of men knew what it took to win.

Missouri was a high-powered team and considered the second best in the Midwest—after Ohio State and ahead of Michigan. In its penultimate game of the season, head coach Dan Devine's Tigers dismantled Kansas 69–21. The 10–1 Tigers tied with Nebraska for the Big 8 title.

The high-scoring Tigers were shut down by the Rover Boys and the rest of Penn State's underappreciated defenders. An inspired defensive effort shook loose and recovered two fumbles and intercepted seven passes thrown by quarterback Terry McMillan. The score looked closer than it was—10–3. Thirty games without a loss. Paterno's Grand Experiment had discovered the proper formula. His first recruiting class was moving on; it would be up to other teams, other eras to add their own ingredients.

When the gun fired to end the game, Charlie, the Rover Boys, and a few dozen more seniors trotted off the field in Miami and headed into Penn State history. They'd built something grand for future players.

The Pro Years

The remainder of his senior year, Charlie possessed something he'd long envied—a normal student's schedule. Magically, he had an extra five to six hours each day as the last months of his college career wound down.

Now that he wasn't being ordered around by the man, Charlie found Paterno a great guy to occasionally visit. It was on one of those visits that Paterno shared what he thought would be a good career choice for his young charge.

"Charlie, you're a smart kid. You should go for your MBA; it will help you in business and I can put in a good word for you wherever you want to go. Harvard's got a good MBA program," Paterno said.

A few years previous, Charlie would have jumped at that offer. But with the career he'd had on the gridiron, there was another level of football awaiting him.

"When I came to Penn State, I had no expectations of playing in the NFL," Pittman remembers. "But I started to get these letters and thought, 'Maybe I should give this a shot.' Joe wanted me to go to Harvard and get my MBA. I really appreciated that. Here is this young coach, in just his third year, who stood to gain more by sending me to the NFL than Harvard. But he told me the NFL could wait. But I thought to myself, 'If I don't give the NFL a shot now, I may never get a chance again.'

"I said to Joe, 'I promise you that I will get my MBA'—and I did get my MBA. I made that commitment."

Bright, personable, and—thanks to Speech 200—well-spoken, Charlie was a star on the national scene with the conclusion of his team's amazing three-year run. After the win against Missouri, Charlie found out quickly about the downside of celebrity.

He was invited to appear on NBC's *Today Show* to be interviewed by host Joe Garagiola. While there, Garagiola asked him what he thought about the NCAA considering expanding the college season to 11 games instead of 10.

"I think that one extra game puts more money in a college's pockets," Charlie said. "But it gives the athletes nothing—except one more game in which to get hurt."

To this day, Charles believes his candor hurt his draft position. But Charlie refused to keep silent if he had an opinion. Unbeaten in high school and college, he felt he had experienced enough in life to speak his mind.

"I went to Mobile, Alabama, to play in the Senior Bowl," Charles recalls. "When I got there, the Dallas Cowboys wanted me to take a test. I said, 'Either I'm good enough to play for you or not. I'm not taking a test.'"

The end of his undergraduate education proved to be a time of rapid change for Charlie. His graduation was on June 10 and on June 27, 1970, he married Mauresé, his high school sweetheart.

"I was supposed to play on the night of my wedding day," he says. "I'm watching an All-Star game on TV on my honeymoon. That game, I was supposed to get the Offensive Player of the Year award, but they gave it to Duane Thomas instead—and then the Cowboys drafted him."

Charlie bypassed the All-Star game to have a honeymoon, but football wasn't too far from his mind.

"Mauresé has got a great arm," he marvels. "She was my quarterback; she was throwing me passes on the beaches of Hawaii."

Charlie was staying in shape for the NFL preseason. He was taken in the third round by the St. Louis Cardinals; he was their fourth selection—they had two second-round picks that year. It was a worrisome selection. At the time, the Cardinals had a poor reputation for their treatment of African American athletes.

"I was having a dynamite camp," he says. "But they wouldn't play me. I remember in one scrimmage, I took the ball from the 30 [yard line] to the two [yard line] and [head coach] Charlie Winner took me out of the game."

If Charlie Pittman's Penn State experience had been charmed, his pro experience was jinxed.

"The pro football experience was initially fantastic," he says. "You're a professional athlete who is idolized all across the country and I was waiting patiently for my turn. It got disappointing for me, especially during the second year. I'd always been a star. I'd been used to being the man. I didn't feel I was getting the proper opportunity to play. One player was blind in one eye and I could outrun him backwards. They cut me and kept him. I was under the illusion that the best athlete played. I didn't know that sometimes you have to keep a certain player just to keep the star athlete happy.

"It became a big disappointment and made me start doubting my own abilities—especially when I didn't get a chance in practice. You don't perform well when you don't get an opportunity. Then you're playing for all the wrong reasons; you're playing not to disappoint your family, fans, and college."

What may seem unfathomable to younger people is the fact that Charlie wasn't rich when he joined the NFL. He played in an era when even some star players had jobs in the off-season to make ends meet.

"My pro career didn't go anywhere near where I wanted to be," he says. "All I did was return kicks and work on special teams for seven games. I was leading the conference in kickoff returns when Charlie Winner comes to me as I'm getting taped. He told me Chuck Latourette was going to be activated and I was going on the taxi squad."

In the NFL, the taxi squad is comprised of the four extra players who are prepared to join the team on short notice, to substitute for injured players. It was not where Charles wanted to be.

"Latourette fumbled kickoffs in the next two games," Charles recalls. "We were 8–2–1 going into it and we didn't win another game. Winner ended up getting fired and management brought in Bob Hollway from the Vikings. He didn't like me, so I was released."

The Baltimore Colts picked up his contract and he was back in his hometown. In his second year in the NFL—1971—things were looking up.

Accorsi had been working behind the scenes in Baltimore to bring Charlie to the Colts.

"I campaigned to claim him," Accorsi says. "But he wasn't the same; he'd gotten bigger."

"That trade was my dream come true," Pittman recalls. "Bubba Smith, Johnny Unitas, John Mackey, Earl Morrall, Glen Ressler— just a dream come true."

Though it was unknown to him, Charlie faced a complicated situation with the Colts—the owner, Carroll Rosenbloom, had sold the team before the season. Accorsi, knowing that some younger players would be unloaded, began to "promote Charlie like crazy." His lobbying efforts were unsuccessful.

"I missed preseason with the Colts because of the roster change," he says. "But when I got there, they never let me carry the ball from scrimmage. I finally got into a game during 'garbage time.' I went 14 yards, got hit, and fumbled the ball. By that time, I hadn't carried the ball for two years. In camp the next season, I'm averaging seven yards a carry. But the coaches come to me and tell me they're going to cut me. Lydell had been drafted by then and they were going to cut both Lydell and me. But [coach/general manager] Joe Thomas intercedes and says, 'You can't cut Lydell,' so they kept him and kept Tom Nowatzke—who ran a 5.4 40-yard dash. I was a 6'1", 205-pound prototype running back and they cut me."

Mitchell dodged that bullet and went on to have an excellent professional career. He never doubted his former teammate had the talent. But at the professional level, he considered him to be too nice of a guy.

"I thought Charlie was a great ballplayer, but probably a little too laid back," Mitchell says. "He was not aggressive, at least not the way I think he should have been. And he had a chronic ankle injury that bothered him. I was never sure he had a tremendous threshold for pain; in the pros, you expect to have injuries.

"He gave the NFL a shot. The thing I like about the guy is that when it was over, he moved on. That is the most difficult thing to do. Some guys destroy everything they've got going for them just to hold on. The NFL is the highest level a football player can reach, and I am proud of having reached it. But at some point, everybody has to move on.

"You do have to have talent; it doesn't happen by accident. Even then, the person who plays 10 hours a day may not make it. Once you do discover your talent, that's just the first step. You have to sacrifice, learn fundamentals, do the proper things. Go that one step beyond. Some guys are afraid to be too good or reach their max. They'll talk it but won't walk the walk. And it's nothing you sit and brag about and gloat about. The example I would give is that young kid [NBA basketball star Dwyane] Wade. He says all the right things, but what he really says—if you listen to him—is he works his behind off."

In 1972, with one-year-old Tony and a flagging career, Charlie had a family to support and decisions to make. He decided to teach high school. That would require a stamina he never knew he had.

He taught ninth and 10th grade at Forest Park High School in Baltimore, Maryland, alma mater of former Maryland governor and United States vice president Spiro Agnew.

"Teaching school was the hardest job I ever had," he recalls. "I had to spend nights staying ahead of students. The girls were tough, especially when they know you're a former NFL football player. I had to put a couple of guys in their places. It seemed like the students I had didn't want to learn history and geography."

During his time of personal upheaval, Charlie visited with his coach. One day they were walking by the murals of past football greats near the weight rooms.

"That's a good picture of Lydell. And a good picture of Franco," Charles teased. "But who's that really handsome guy there?"

"Is that you up there, Charlie? They must have made a mistake," Paterno said. "I'll get somebody to take it down."

"Well, Joe, I'll tell you one thing, without that guy," he said, pointing to his own picture, "you don't get that guy, or that guy, or that guy."

Paterno chuckled.

"So, how are you doing Charlie?"

"I'm okay," he shrugged. "You know I got cut by Baltimore. I'm thinking I might try Canada. I hear their football is getting pretty good."

Paterno paused and put his hand on Charlie's shoulder.

"Charlie, you're playing to prove your college career wasn't a fluke," Paterno said. "You don't have anything to prove to anybody. It might be time to let it go."

Paterno let his words sink in, before adding, "I've got a friend, Ted Junker, who might be able to get you a job at a bank. Let me call him for you."

Charles was both devastated and relieved. He knew deep inside that Joe was right. He realized that he viewed college football and NFL football the same way.

"The reason I wasn't successful in the pros is because I didn't understand the different nature of a team. You've got to make your teammates better in the pros," he says. "I thought my ability to run and catch a football was enough. But if I don't make my teammates better, it doesn't matter what kind of ability I have. I'd be in the locker room and I'd just be there. Everyone else would be socializing while I'm learning the plays, studying my playbooks. How is that making Tom Matte or John Unitas trust me as a teammate? They don't know me. Why keep me? I'm not making anyone better. I'm not supplying the synergy required."

Charlie wasn't sure he wanted to expend the energy anymore. It wasn't fun anymore; it had become a job.

"When Joe said, 'Get on with your life,' I made the decision to do just that. For a while, I was in denial. It's difficult when your career finally ends. I'd been doing it for 12 to 15 years. The fame, the notoriety, it's hard to walk away from. It used to pain me—personally—to see the people I used to play with still playing. So I didn't watch professional football for a year."

Charlie called Paterno and agreed to the interview, which led to a job he held for seven years at Marine Bank in Erie.

Down to Business   Knowing when to let go is one of the hardest lessons to learn, not just in business, but in life. It feels like betrayal, or abandonment, or sorrow. Sometimes it feels like all of those rolled in one. Charlie's decision to end his NFL career is a case in point.

Lydell Mitchell spoke one of life's most poignant truths when he said, "At some point, everybody has to move on."

When the Fire Dies

We're not talking about course corrections; we're not talking about second-guessing. We are talking about turning away from something that you have poured sweat and tears into. Charlie was lucky enough to know it was time to go for two reasons: a caring mentor, and the realization that he didn't have the passion anymore.

We quote Mitchell once more: "Some guys destroy everything they've got going for them just to hold on."

Finding One's Direction

Tony Pittman knows when he has arrived at a company that fits. "I look for the mission; it means something to have it written down. I read it and look for clues about the company. Consistency is a big clue. I ask whether a company is on the upswing or in recovery mode. When there are varying opinions of that, that's a clue.

"There should be consistency of message, of views. Those are at least threads to follow. I'm a big believer that organizations reflect the personalities and styles of top leadership. That may become less of a factor in today's world. For example, there were a lot of people at my former employer [IBM] who worked at home, got their assignments online, and were detached from the personalities at the office. Still, companies with dominant personalities are out there. One that comes to mind is Apple— Steve Jobs, that company is his. His view of technology as art and being different by being more innovative infuses every aspect of that company. He's become an icon and the company is wrapped around his personality. Bill Gates and Microsoft used to be that way."

In today's workplace, corporations—and personalities—are going to have to adapt to new realities presented by the workforce, Tony says, "Companies who don't quite get it, they can still kind of still get away with it, but they're probably not aware of the tumult that awaits them down the road. They'll have butts in the seats for now, but in 10 years they'll fall behind because the best and brightest aren't interested in what they have to offer."

Assess Team Dynamics

"Whenever I'm part of a work group, whether I'm leading it or a key contributor, I work to understand the dynamics of the team. I'm used to making quick assessments of other individuals, checking their 'need' and 'crave' buttons," Tony says. "I'm not directing or pushing. I just want to understand the egos. Everyone wants to feel important and feel they are making a meaningful contribution.

"So a leader might want to acknowledge in groups, in some small way, those contributions. It's good to know who you're working with and what floats their boat. You're not going to define it; they've already defined it, you just have to find out what it is—find the button and push it when necessary. I've noticed that not a lot of managers know how to do that. I learned it a long time ago. My father was my soccer coach and I always was fascinated by how he treated different kids different ways to motivate them.

"I used to work in the semiconductor business with IBM and we had customers with complex needs like Microsoft. In some instances, I ran into very deep, very intelligent individuals who liked to talk more than they liked to listen. They had this wealth of technical information that they needed to get out. They loved to be heard by a business guy who was not a Jedi master of chip development. Others needed to be paraded out in front of people to get involved. How do you assess that? Use probing questions, observe people in meetings; see what perks them up and what makes them sit back and not participate in a meeting."

> **WINNING IN LIFE**
> "No matter how great you are, you will always be remembered for your last worst act. Bill Clinton, Richard Nixon, Mike Tyson, Kobe Bryant, Pete Rose, O.J. Simpson. All of them did great things and maybe thought their fame would let them get away with something. It won't. I try to live my life remembering that one bad act can destroy everything I've built."
> —*Charles Pittman*

CHAPTER 9

Ready, Steady, Go!

In 1994, when the Lions took the home field against the Northwestern Wildcats, it had been a long season full of ups and downs. The upside was spectacular in that all the guys were concentrating on winning. The downside was that winning wasn't enough to get the team to its desired destination at the top of the polls. Despite beating ranked opponents Michigan, Southern Cal, and Ohio State, their perfect season was considered to be worth only a number two ranking.

For nonathletes, it's hard to grasp how deeply disappointing it is to not be ranked number one when all evidence seems to point to that conclusion. College athletes occupy a fast-moving moment in time they will never get back. Lost championships are an amalgam of summer love affairs, botched promotions, and missed flights; just one big perplexing bog of emotions.

Fifth-year seniors like Tony push those feelings to the side come game time. But the possibilities occupy their waking moments during the week.

Despite being in their early twenties, seniors who have a year like Penn State did in 1994 cherish those moments as deeply as senior citizens recalling their youth: *This is my last game on this field. This will be the last time I see these guys.* Football can engender quite tender memories for such a rough sport, which is probably the reason one wit considered such reveries "a nostalgic punch in the mouth."

The memories it freezes into your mind often aren't Hallmark card material.

"I remember Mark D'Onofrio from when I was a freshman," Tony recalls. "He was the starting middle linebacker and before every game he had to throw up a couple of times. That was how he got ready to play, and he'd be crazy on the field."

Still, memories weren't going to beat Northwestern, or Michigan State the week after that. The work, as ever, was done on the field. And Paterno was cranky for a winning coach. With 14 wins in a row, he was nearly halfway to his zenith, the 30-game unbeaten streak Charlie Pittman and his teammates had enjoyed. Winning always seemed to add another layer to Paterno's machinations. He had to make sure there weren't let-downs or overconfidence.

"We were very well prepared for Northwestern," Pittman recalls. "The Wildcats really weren't very good. I remember them trying a double reverse, and we just nailed it. They weren't going to beat us with trickery, that was for sure."

As usual, the offense performed at full bore. Between Ki-Jana Carter's running and Kerry Collins's passing, the game was nearly out of reach by halftime. The final score was 45–17.

"The key to success for this game, and really our entire schedule that year, was to be smart," Tony says. "That was what I focused on. We didn't have to have a defense that would go out and create turnovers. If we played smart we would win. I viewed my job as not being stupid, not getting fooled. That was my mind-set. You have to know when to play like that, and I believe that one of my talents was an ability to play smart team football."

Rubin, who graduated in 1993, was Pittman's sponsor on his recruiting trip to Penn State and the pair became—and remain—close friends. He said the hardest thing about preparing for big games were the off-field distractions; he credited Tony with being able to ignore them.

"The really tough games are the ones with all the media attention," Rubin says. "The interviews: ESPN, ABC, there can be so much hype it's hard to stay focused. Hype doesn't help you make a tackle. Michigan, Ohio State, those were big games. The challenge for us was to stay focused and play football. Tony was a very thoughtful guy; one of our cover corners. He was out there on the island and wasn't responsible for much other than covering the other team's best wide receiver. Cover corners are different breeds. They don't want to be bothered and typically they have pretty robust egos. It's pride and ego that make them good cover corners. Tony's attitude was, 'Tell me what I need to know and let me do it.'"

With the Lions' win against Northwestern, all that was left in the regular season was the game against the Michigan State Spartans—and it would be off to the Rose Bowl.

The Lions' offense popped off another high-scoring affair and beat the Spartans by a score of 59–31. Tony and the Lions were smelling roses. Who knows? Maybe even a national championship would be in the offing.

No tackle had ever stung as much. Charles was in the office of Ted Junker, a man he considered a friend and a mentor in the banking industry. Junker had taken him into the field seven years prior when he had no experience. Charles had taught himself much about the banking industry and earned Junker's trust. But that didn't matter. Junker was doing what he had to do as a bank president. Charles had gone past the guidelines in trying to help a business. When the business went delinquent on its loans and Charles tried to hide it to give the business more time to succeed, it looked bad for the bank, for Junker—and Charles would have to be let go.

At 32, with a wife and three children, Charles was unemployed. He had feared failure for so long that faced with it in this situation, it felt like he could hardly breathe. Compounding the pain was the fact that Joe Paterno had recommended him for the job.

I let both Joe and Ted down, Charles thought, feeling miserable. In the tradition of "no good deed goes unpunished," he gained nothing from the transaction that cost him his job. He was just trying to help a struggling African American business.

Charles knew what he had to do, but he surely didn't want to do it. After he called Mauresé to let her know, he had to call Paterno and tell him.

"I was terrified of failure," he recalls. "But I had fallen and I had to bounce back. I'd been knocked down pretty badly. I had to get up and play through it. But a failure of this magnitude? It was very difficult to call Joe, but I did. I told him I failed him and disappointed a Penn State guy [Junker]. Joe said to come see him. He said he would help me find a job somewhere else."

Charles met with Joe just before Christmas 1980. Just seeing his old coach at that time of year was unusual. Penn Staters knew not to try to contact Paterno around bowl season; he was too focused. Joe told Charles that he had contacted Ed Mead, the president of the *Erie Times-News* and set up a meeting.

"Thank you, Joe," Charles said as he prepared to leave.

"Charlie," Joe said. "How's the family? Mauresé, Tony, Mauresa, and Kira?"

"They're fine, Joe," he replied.

"Charles was a great hire for us," says Ed Mead. "He came in and explained what happened with Marine Bank. I told him, 'That doesn't concern us. I'm glad you told me, but that doesn't concern me.'

"We were looking for a promotion manager," Mead says, "and my son knew him pretty well. He said he'd do a good job. And he was right. Among other things, Charlie is a great people person. He'd gotten well-known in Erie as a guy who liked people. Ted told me he didn't want to let him go; he had to. It didn't color my perceptions at all."

Mead is a gregarious man whose family business has been a mainstay in the Erie area since 1888. He also possessed an elite athletic pedigree: he was captain of the Princeton football team in 1948.

Charles's personality was a strong selling point when he interviewed for the position. Mead had to find someone who would fit and appreciated the unique position his publications held in the area.

"We're a family-owned newspaper; we feel we are the conscience of the community. I explained that to Charles and he liked that," Mead says.

Mead hired him in 1981 and Charles spent 10 years with the family-owned chain.

"They hired me as marketing/promotions director," Charles recalls. "It was ideally suited for me. I had to improve their brand, get their message out. We wanted people to do business with us not because they had to—because they wanted to. We wanted people to feel like they had choices whether they had them or not. A newspaper should love its community and not be afraid to wrap its arms around the community and be a community's best friend.

"We did more to make people feel like their paper worked hard for them. We had service awards, weekly newsletters. People began to feel like they wanted to work at our newspaper. Circulation grew, name recognition grew, employee satisfaction increased. We made sure we gave birthday cards and gifts to our employees. I did that job for two years and then became the classified ad manager. We became the fastest growing ad sections in the state."

Charles also wrote a sports column that focused on the social ramifications of sports. His time at the *Erie Times-News* put ink in his blood.

"I wanted to be a newspaper publisher, which would have been difficult in a family-owned company," Charles says. "In the meantime, they brought in an ad director who I had to report to; it was another layer of management, which meant I was further away from being a publisher. The ad director was a nice guy, but not really in tune with political correctness. I talked to the Meads about it and let them know I was looking to be a publisher."

Charles decided to join the Knight-Ridder's executive training program for general executives at the *Charlotte Observer*. He was 43 and it was a five-year program. Tony was in his second year at Penn State.

"I was sorry to see Charles go," Mead says. "Whenever an issue came up, Charles was prepared. He was well organized. The big thing was Charles could get along with people. In our business, that's very important. Sometimes you run into people who are still carrying their competence on their sleeve. He knew he was good, but he worked with people without putting that distance between them.

"I consider Charlie a very good friend. We have a good relationship. I'm a great admirer of Charles, I've seen what he can do; I've seen his dedication to his kids, his mother. He's just one hell of a good guy. He's one of those guys you instantly like. You can talk straight. You can talk race with Charles and he talks back."

Publisher Rolfe Neill, who would be Charles's champion at the *Charlotte Observer*, believed in working on a person's weaknesses and turning them into strengths. Charles had a different opinion. He believed businesspeople should work on their strengths and simply shore up their weaknesses.

"We were trying to make Charles into an all-purpose executive," Neill explains. "I really believe that leadership ability is something that translates into any setting. My theory is you can take a smart person, whatever their weaknesses are; those weaknesses will dissipate or go away. The idea was to give an intelligent guy a place where he could blossom despite not knowing anything about the job we put him in. Theoretically, I was in charge of everything, but I couldn't have known every aspect of the process."

Neill said his greatest appreciation of Charles came from his ability to tell the truth to those above him in the corporate structure.

"There is a serenity in Charles that is inspiring," he says. "I think it is as literal as that—he tells the truth. Always speaks the truth. The top of any good-size organization is tremendously isolated; there is a lot you should know about how to run a business better that won't reach you if don't establish an atmosphere where it's safe to tell the truth."

For his part, Charles was concerned that he was approaching 50 years of age and was still in the training program.

"The closer it got to the end of the five years, the more nervous I got," he said. "I wanted to see some signs that I was closer to getting to be a publisher. I'm thinking that I'm getting closer to 50 and I shouldn't be in training. About that time, the publisher's job in State College became available. Rolfe Neill wanted me to apply for the ad director position.

"Even though it wasn't a publisher's job, Neill made it clear that it would be a good position to achieve if I wanted to be a publisher. So I went in knowing I wasn't going for a publisher's job. But I got the impression they didn't want me in that position, either."

Charles made clear his intention that he wanted the position as ad director. But he wasn't positive the company was trying hard enough to recruit him. While at a basketball game with Paterno, he made up his mind to call the company's personnel department the next chance he got. He later spoke with a manager at the publication and told her he didn't feel they were pursuing him with any kind of diligence. While on that conversation, he decided to meet with the personnel director.

A week after meeting with her, they called him with the news they would be making the offer to someone else.

Charles then interviewed with Davenport, Iowa–based Lee Enterprises for a publisher's position; the interview went well and Lee executives were impressed with the skills he could bring to their operation. Lee, founded in 1890, is the fourth-largest newspaper group in America. It is a publicly traded media company that publishes 58 daily newspapers in 23 states, as well as 300 weekly, classified, and specialty publications. The company also provides online services, including websites supporting its daily newspapers and certain of its other publications. The company acquired Pulitzer Inc., the company that awards the coveted prizes, in 2005. It would be the largest newspaper group for which Charles ever worked.

The next day, he spoke with the company's president, Dick Gottlieb, and told them he was ready to accept the offer. It was his first job as a publisher—with the Decatur, Illinois, newspaper *Herald & Review*.

"I had been doing what others wanted me to do. But I wanted to succeed in business, so I had to set my own goals," Charles recalls. "There were times that I had to really pinch myself and remember how far I'd come. When I was publisher in Decatur, Dwayne Andreas, the president of ADM, wanted to meet with me. I went to his office."

Andreas's office, located on East Faries Parkway in Decatur, was all that the office of the CEO of a $35-billion-a-year company should be: well-appointed, tasteful, strangely quiet—and big.

Archer Daniels Midland Company (ADM) is a world leader in agricultural processing and fermentation technology. It is one of the world's largest processors of soybeans, corn, wheat, and cocoa, and also a leader in the production of soybean oil and meal, ethanol, corn sweeteners, and flour. The man whom Charles was chatting with oversaw a workforce of 25,000 employees with more than 250 processing plants.

"While I was there, I couldn't help but say to him, 'Wow, my mother would be so impressed to know I was in your office and that you and I would be working together.'"

It had been a long trek from 824 Appleton Street.

Down to Business   "Discipline, structure, toughness. That's football and it's business," says Lee Rubin. "I really believe that Joe consciously wasn't just preparing us for Saturday's game, he was preparing us for life. Joe has a very healthy sensitivity for other cultures. That bled over into the team; it was one of the interesting things we had going on. People have always had issues with race, Joe would explain to us that coming up, he was considered very ethnic. Wasps didn't want a guy with an *O* at the end of his name to be coaching."

Always Obstacles

"He wasn't trying to compare being Italian to being black," said Lee Rubin. "He was letting us know there are always going to be obstacles; always going to be barriers. He's just that type of human being; he'll tell you honestly what's going on. I like to think we all came away a little more aware. I think, for instance, a guy like Paul Posluszny, I would want him on my football team. I don't care what color he is. I played with Mark D'Onofrio, who is a really good linebacker. What sports does is blur those [racial] lines because winning becomes the thing."

Don't Burn Bridges

Charles believes that relationships are the lingua franca of business, and the incident he considers his greatest business failure wasn't a total failure.

"Ted Junker and I are still friends," he says. "He realized I made a bad decision while trying to do something good. The best thing about the situation is that Penn State relationship is still there; I never burned the bridge."

If You Have a Team Sports Background, Use It to Frame Your Goal Setting

"That whole perspective has helped me," says Tony Pittman. "Day to day in the business world, I'll be sitting in meetings and I can sometimes see my coworkers drifting away from what the goal is. No one thinks to ask, why are we doing [this project]? We can never forget why. It should almost be a daily affirmation. But not everyone has the makeup or past experience to keep that focus.

"I believe there are plenty of people who have it in them, but it may not have been brought out. On a high-functioning team, people know: day by day, did we get closer to the goal or farther away?"

In business, "team" is a murky concept; in a workgroup there might be five or six people from a consulting firm, others might be intra-company but borrowed from other divisions.

"[While I was at IBM] I was involved with the supply chain initiatives. Our goal was to generate significant bottom-line savings for the company," Tony recalls. "My goal was to work on what my team had to do in order to do its part. The sports analogy is, we want to go 12–0 and be national champs. Of course, that's understood as long-range goal setting. Good leaders get you focused on what you have to do now. At Penn State, did I have a goal to lead the team in interceptions? No. That wasn't a goal. And at no time did Joe, during a 12–0 season, say, 'You guys can be national champions.' We were intent on getting better at what each of us did—every day."

> **WINNING IN LIFE**
>
> "The skills that got you into your position are going to be much different than upper-level management skills. It's a whole different world between being good at what you do and leading people into being good at what they do. Ask this question of yourself: what do I really want out of being upper-level management? Is it just because it looks like the place to go? What if you are really suited to being a master of a certain process? People should think about what they want to do. At any given company there are only two or three top-level people. What's your plan B? Or plan C? For instance, if someone wants to be the CEO of IBM, every IBM CEO has, at some point, made a big mark in generating sales. So, to achieve that goal, you'd better start selling...fast!"
>
> —*Tony Pittman*

CHAPTER 10

Your Own Grand Experiment

Twenty-five years and one day after his father walked off the turf of the Orange Bowl for the last time as a Nittany Lion, Tony traversed that same last mile. He trudged off the field of the Rose Bowl, tired, sweaty, and with a lump in his throat. The Lions had just defeated 12th-ranked Oregon, 38–20, and run the table on a perfect season.

Tony will always remember that moment. The setting could pass for a fairy tale if not for the aroma of exhaust fumes and blaring car horns. The Rose Bowl sits in a verdant corner of Arroyo Seco called Brookside Park; just north of Pasadena's breathtaking Colorado Street Bridge, a 15-story concrete arch bridge that spans the Arroyo. The bridge is a distinctive 1,486-foot-long structure with Beaux Arts arches, retro light standards, and railings that look too gossamer to hold streams of cars. It is a landmark listed on the National Register of Historic Places. Parallel to the ethereal bridge, a river of traffic on the nearby Foothills Freeway provided a red and white light show as Tony closed out his college career with a streak of 15 victories as a starter.

The Pittman record was set: 45 games started without a single loss.

Tony and his teammates had comprised a team for ages, but college is a way station for most and it was time to move on. Only Paterno stayed. His staff would spend another year casting about for more kids with sharp minds and world-class athleticism. Tony's day was done.

It had been a long road to this pinnacle. It had taken every shred of his patience and desire to contribute to something as grand as Penn State's 1994 football program. He had volunteered for an extra year of prep school, redshirted a year in college, endured injuries that would have cowed a man with a lower pain threshold.

All that sacrifice had weighed on his mind the night before the Rose Bowl showdown as he and his teammates watched television in their downtown Los Angeles hotel. They were hoping against hope that Miami—the anti–Penn State—could beat Nebraska in the Orange Bowl.

For a while it looked good. Miami started the fourth quarter with a 17–9 lead over the Cornhuskers and even had a spectacular interception by Earl Little. Tony and his teammates shouted encouragement at the TV, but Miami wouldn't score again. The Cornhuskers and their beloved coach would win 24–17 and be crowned national champions.

Tony's personal rewards for his diligence would include second-team All–Big Ten selection and first-team Academic All-American. The university awarded him its Oswald Award as Penn State's most outstanding scholar-athlete and the O'Hora Award for exemplary conduct and improvement, and the National Football Foundation and College Football Hall of Fame also honored him as a scholar-athlete.

Now came the hard part for anyone who was a starter at a program like Penn State: was it time to go to the pros?

"I got that question a lot," says Tony. "When I sat down and decided to go to Penn State, I remember saying to myself, it's not because of being able to go pro from there. The prospect of playing in the NFL is the equivalent of going out and buying a few lottery tickets. The odds are staggering against winning.

"There are guys with way more talent than me, but they never made it into the starting lineup at Penn State. It's even more of a long shot to make it in the pros. If you're smart, you don't want to bet too much on it. I was sitting in a restaurant with Joe having that conversation when he was recruiting me. Joe said, 'You may never be an NFL player,' and I told him, 'I'm okay with that, just let me be a Penn State player.'

"But when I walked off the Rose Bowl's field, I thought to myself, 'Are you really okay with that?' A few days later, on a Tuesday afternoon, NFL scouts were waiting for me to work out for them on campus and I'm sitting around thinking whether I should go for it or not. I'd heard a lot from my teammates, from my father. All of them said don't pursue the NFL if you don't have tunnel vision. I mentioned my dilemma to Dave Thomas, a big defensive lineman from Maryland. He said, 'You're lucky you can make that decision. A lot of guys put themselves in a hole; they don't give themselves any other options.'

"I didn't have to do that. I was just trying to figure out the likelihood of turning it into a life-fulfilling career. I had already sustained some injuries playing college ball. It occurred to me that one can't buy body parts to replace what's been damaged. Joe and I went to the Waldorf Hotel to receive an award, and I got a chance to see a bunch of football greats; I remember Tony Dorsett was there. These guys would go to stand up, and they couldn't. There were guys who once could do anything on a football field, and now they were hobbling around the hotel. Joe remarked, "This is one of the things that does not 'light me up' about football. Your quality of life is impacted. Having a parent who played, I knew a lot more than just what was it was like when I turned on my TV."

Knowing that his passion for the game didn't burn hot enough to justify an attempt at the NFL, Tony began his business career.

Charles rose to become senior vice-president at Lee Enterprises and remained there for six years. He left when he was asked to cut 20 people's positions. In his mind, that violated one of his firmest principles—loyalty. He would have preferred to find another way to increase shareholder value in this instance.

"There are certain beliefs and values that I just won't violate," he said. "A Lee executive wanted me to cut 20 people, and I told him I couldn't do it without his considering better alternatives that I had offered. He said, 'Well, you have to do it.' I said, 'No, I don't. Because I quit.'

"[Lee president] Mary Junck and I met the next day. She came to my office and I explained my position to her. She said, 'Charles, we'll move you to Carlisle [Pennsylvania]. That's closer to home for you and even closer to Penn State.' She asked me to take a week, go visit Carlisle, and get back to her. I went there, checked it out, and got back to her right away.

"I told her it wouldn't be fair to the community or to the employees in Carlisle if I took a position on a temporary basis until I found something better. I talked it out with Mauresé, and then I quit without a job in hand. During that week I started feeling around. It's not as if I walked out into the cold. I had my reputation, my track record. Within three weeks, I had a job. I quit in June at Lee, found a job in July with Schurz Communications, and started there in August."

Jim Schurz, chair of Schurz Communications, said he felt as if a four-leaf clover had fallen into his hands.

"He came highly recommended. He let some folks know he wasn't totally happy at Lee; he had worked for family newspapers and he preferred to work for a family. I knew his track record and I was impressed by him. His first newspaper employment was in Pennsylvania, so I called and asked around," Schurz said. "A friend of mine said if you have a shot at him, go for him."

It wasn't the first time the two had met.

"I remember meeting him at a function in San Diego," Schurz said. "Charlie came in and sat down and ordered a Coke and maraschino cherries—he loves maraschino cherries. We chatted then, and that was mostly social. He was very bright, very focused, and highly motivated. He is just used to succeeding.

"We're very much on the same wavelength; when we came against people who were squeezing the bottom line, they were generally accountants or lawyers and we recognized that there might be other courses of action. I literally turned the reins over to Charles when he came on board. His workers have nothing but praise for him; to the point where I wonder what I did wrong when I had the job."

Down to Business	One of the key skill sets for any successful businessperson is knowing how to listen first, says Tony Pittman.

Three Rules of Being a Successful Listener
First Rule: Find the "Ticker"
Learn how to understand what makes people around you tick. That's the key to your success. Don't always try to speak first. Go into challenging situations with ears open, not with an open mouth, Tony recommends.

Second Rule: Be a Salesperson
"It's not just listening, but listening to what matters. There is an element of salesmanship, no matter what role you have: you have to be good at selling people ideas. Selling in its many different incarnations is the lifeblood of business."

Third Rule: Avoid Being an Office Gossip
"My instinct for this kind of thing is: don't participate," he says. "Don't indulge in the 'I've got to get something on someone to get in the game' mentality. Avoid those side conversations in hallways, corners. Don't get involved. Be a breath of fresh air; be fact-based.

Accept no emotionally unintelligent conversations. Your question should always be, 'What are the current relevant facts and how will it affect our business?'"

> **WINNING IN LIFE**
> "People without an athletic background too often play not to lose; I play to win. You don't wait until everything is flowing at 100 percent—you take a calculated risk. You push harder. You don't want to fail, so you don't have an expectation to lose. In a win-win situation, when you're successful, your customer wins. And you should never win at the cost of your employees or vendors. Do this and your reputation grows in the industry. Promotion opportunities come your way. Your customer base increases and you're learning how to succeed."
> —*Charles Pittman*

CHAPTER 11

Undefeated in Life

"It wasn't comfortable at first strapping on the pads," Tony Pittman recalls. "I thought to myself, 'What is this guy coming after me trying to do?' Football teaches you to become like my friend Phil Collins's brother Andre. Andre went to the pros, and Phil has a poster showing Andre mauling Warren Moon. Andre signed the picture, 'Sometimes you have to go for the face.' On the field, you have to become someone else for those three or four hours. You have to. In the business world you have to do that, too. To be successful, you have to become someone else in certain situations. And sometimes you have to refuse to be victimized."

One of the themes of *Playing for Paterno* is the arbitrary nature of success. Despite playing on three of Joe Paterno's five undefeated squads, neither Charlie nor Tony Pittman ever won a national championship. They lost no games as starters, and yet the big prize eluded them.

It brings to mind an old video featuring Beatle Paul McCartney called "Coming Up." McCartney plays a bunch of musical scamps and scalawags from the 1960s and 1970s. One of the most endearing of his characters is his hippie sax player, who is perfectly out of sync with the other three members of the horn section: they go up, he goes down; they go forward, he goes back.

For the Pittmans, that was what dreams of national championships must have felt like. But there is a common sentiment spoken by both of the men—they didn't miss a thing.

It is safe to say that both Tony and Charles loved their Penn State experiences. It provided an education, it helped them make friends for life, and it taught them both valuable lessons about the real textures of winning and losing.

"I came to Penn State as very shy young man," Charles said in a speech in 2003. "I hadn't been exposed to much outside of my little neighborhood. I became a football All-American, I went on to get my MBA, I helped the program by helping to recruit more black students like Lydell Mitchell and Franco Harris. And for a while, I was telling people that I had done more for Penn State than it had done for me—and I was wrong. Penn State did more for me than I could ever do for Penn State."

A great part of that experience had to do with Joe Paterno. Paterno is a hard man to play for—like any college coach—because he has to be dispassionate about his talent. But when an athlete's playing days are over, that's when he becomes closer to a father figure for his charges. Lydell Mitchell still speaks highly of both Paterno and his program.

"In anything in life, whether it's in business or sports, if you want to succeed you have to adhere to the fundamentals," Mitchell says. "You have to really understand and learn them. You need breaks along the way, sure; it doesn't hurt to have a break here and there. But more than anything, we learned a lot from Joe. He kept our feet on the ground. He made us pay attention to the smallest details. Teams didn't beat us mentally. We didn't make mistakes over and over again. We could always go back and think about things we accomplished when a crisis came up, so there would be no need to panic. We always kept our cool. Joe shared his philosophy—don't get too satisfied with what you're doing, because then you have problems. The goal is to try and get better every single day. If you're able to do that, no matter what, you'll be successful. Transfer that knowledge to a couple of generations of Penn State players and you'll understand the success of our program. There is no magic. The main thing is we have that basic habit. We prepare ourselves."

There's an old joke about an out-of-towner asking a New Yorker how to get to Carnegie Hall. The reply is: practice. Getting to be part of the Penn State football program, even in spirit, has the same answer.

If you're a football fan, by all means, go back and read the accounts of the games; they're amazing bits of drama. But here's a secret: every one of those games could be used as a lesson for business. Overconfidence? Read the passage about the 1968 game against Kansas State. Unforeseen circumstances? Check out the Illinois game in 1994. Powerful opponent? Michigan 1994. Overcoming adversity? Syracuse 1969. Lack of confidence? That's not in the program—just as it shouldn't be in yours.

Football and business are endeavors that acolytes learn over the course of time. The more they learn, the more they find they don't know. Charles, for instance, had to learn that being a good teammate meant something different at each level of the game. Despite being in his mid-twenties in the NFL, he had no clue how that game worked.

Every day offers you opportunities for growth, if you're receptive. Go back and read the "Down to Business" sections of each chapter. Notice how often the themes of preparation, practice, and belief come up—either alone or in conjunction with other concepts. That is your bedrock for your own undefeated life. It forms a closed loop: if you prepare, you have to study the situation; if you study the situation, you know what is feasible; if you know what is feasible, you practice for success; if you practice enough, you are confident; if you're confident, you succeed; if you succeed, you believe in your abilities; and if you believe in your abilities, you prepare for more success.

Charles and Tony Pittman have lived that rare dream of elite athletes who have gone on to do great things in business as well. Over the years, they've come to realize that being a business success comes down to four very basic agreements, as coined by Don Miguel Ruiz and Don Jose Ruiz, that you make with yourself:

1. Be impeccable with your word—Speak with integrity; say only what you mean.

2. Always do your best—Your best is going to change from moment to moment.

3. Never make assumptions—Find the courage to ask questions and to express what you really want.

4. Never take things personally—Nothing others do is because of you; it is a projection of their own reality.

As promised, you've been in the locker rooms, on the practice fields, and inside the boardrooms of the Pittmans' lives. Now that you have the concepts down, it's time to do what real football players—and businesspeople—do: practice. Remember, anything you can do after one attempt is not a skill, it's just a movement.

See you on the other side of the Blue Line!

Down to Business "There's a saying that goes 'Experience is a tough teacher; the test comes before the lesson.' Leaving the sports world and entering the business world is a difficult lesson to learn. Having talked to and known a lot of ex-athletes who entered the business world, the fundamental change in the team concept is the most difficult thing for them to overcome. In sports, there's this 'hey, I'll watch your back' mentality; there is camaraderie. In the business world, it's not always that way. Sometimes it's a matter of 'I'll watch your back to a point, but if something tough comes along, I may get out of the way so I don't have to deal with the difficult issues.' In large companies people are more than okay with that: 'Oops, that guy got hit, but hey, at least it wasn't me.' I've worked with people whose only objective was to avoid getting hit. In the sports world, that's like going into the game-plan meeting and saying, 'Hoo boy! I hope they don't call any plays for me.' Tell me a successful team that really succeeds that way? A lot of people with backgrounds like mine will fall into the trap of taking all the weight. Those people should be aware that they're not helping to create a team either."

—*Tony Pittman*

Afterword

In his initial contact with me, Charlie Pittman asked me to excuse the fact that he was talking like a proud papa. He told me that his son Tony was an excellent student, athlete, and person, and that if Tony got the opportunity to attend Phillips Academy to play for the Big Blue, we wouldn't be disappointed.

As a varsity coach at Andover, it is not uncommon to hear from proud parents of potential students. Charlie's comments were extraordinary because, despite his own superlative résumé, he never mentioned himself. He only spoke on behalf of his son. But Charlie was indeed impressive. He had distinguished himself at Penn State and nationally not only as an athletic talent but as an academic one as well. Charlie told me that his son was talented, humble, studious, and a model citizen. In fact, Tony sounded a great deal like the Charlie Pittman I had read about. Charlie's comments about Tony weren't boastful or vain. They were said as information: simply stating the facts. The fact that Charlie never mentioned his own pedigree just added to the weight of his words. Two years later, at graduation, I was able to tell Charlie that not only had Tony lived up to his advanced billing, he had exceeded it.

On campus Tony became the model of what a student athlete should be. In athletics, great athletes make those around them better. Tony took that a step further. As a great person, he made our entire campus community better. At Andover, the school's motto is *non sibi*—not for self. The Pittman family lives this motto every day, working and living to make the community better. Tony worked the program in every aspect. He was a tireless honor student, a conscientious and always helpful citizen, and a tremendous three-sport athlete (football, basketball, and track). The hallmark of Tony's success here at Andover was that he never cut corners, literally or figuratively. I observed Tony crossing campus. Many students cut across the lawn—Tony never did. He stuck to the paths. Tony simply does things the right way, not the easy way.

In addition to being Tony's coach, I was his house counselor. In the dormitory setting, a great deal is revealed about a person. Many students with gridiron glory like to be Big Man on Campus, but not Tony. It was common to see Tony taking out the trash after a pizza party. Why? Because it needed to be done. Tony worked and played with his dorm mates with the same enthusiasm and zeal he showed his teammates. He was the glue that brought our diverse dorm together.

As it turns out, Charlie was a man of his word. Tony was indeed all his father promised. On the field he had no peer, rushing for more than 1,000 yards in both of his seasons. To this day, some of Tony's long runs are still marveled at. One of his most memorable was a twisting change of direction, a tackle-breaking 70-yard adventure during a "nor'easter" downpour. The run itself was a highlight film, and in typical Tony fashion, when he crossed the goal line, he just stopped. No jumping up and down, no end-zone celebration, just on to the next thing.

In June 1990, Tony graduated from Phillips Academy in Andover with one of the school's highest prizes, the Yale Bowl, which is "given to the member of the senior class who has attained the highest proficiency in scholarship and athletics." In hindsight, it is apparent that Charlie was being humble. Tony was much more than we expected. He became the standard-bearer, the poster boy, and the role model for what we want our student-athletes to be.

Tony was a highly recruited athlete. However, only the schools with solid academic records could come calling, as the world knew that academics came first in the Pittman home. At one point, on one of his visits to Andover, President George Bush (Andover class of 1941) wanted to say hi to Tony on behalf of Yale. I recall thinking, "Wow, the president! Who would Notre Dame send, the pope?" In the end it didn't matter because JoePa beckoned. Tony was going home to follow in his father's footsteps to play for the most storied and successful coach in college history.

—Leon Modeste